HAL LEONARD BANJO CHORD FINDER

by CHAD JOHNSON

Introduction

Banjo Chord Finder is an extensive reference guide to over 2,800 chords, covering four of the most commonly used tunings. Thirty different chord qualities are covered for each key, and each chord quality is presented in two different voicings. Open strings are used when possible, but one voicing from each quality will be a moveable form. This allows for many unique voicings but also provides practical chord forms that can be transposed to any key.

ISBN 978-0-634-05429-7

HAL•LEONARD® CORPORATION

7777 W. BLUEMOUND RD. P.O. BOX 13819 MILWAUKEE, WI 53213

In Australia Contact:
Hal Leonard Australia Pty. Ltd.
22 Taunton Drive P.O. Box 5130
Cheltenham East, 3192 Victoria, Australia
Email: ausadmin@halleonard.com

Visit Hal Leonard Online at
www.halleonard.com

TABLE OF CONTENTS

FRETBOARD DIAGRAMS

A fingerboard chart of the banjo neck in each tuning is provided below for reference.

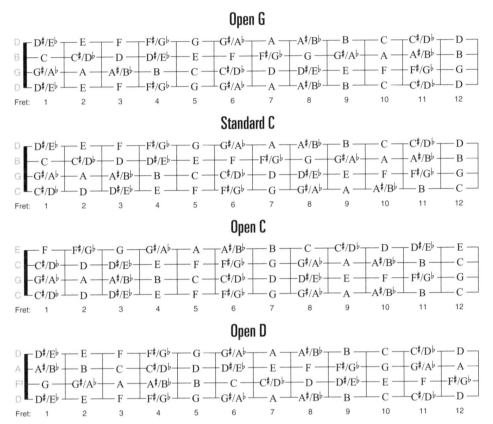

Open G

Standard C

Open C

Open D

The chords throughout this book are presented in chord grid fashion. In case you're not familiar with this type of notation, below is a detailed explanation of how they're read. The four vertical lines represent the four strings on the banjo. They are arranged low to high from left to right.

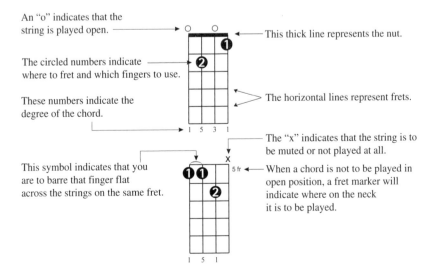

An "o" indicates that the string is played open. → This thick line represents the nut.

The circled numbers indicate where to fret and which fingers to use.

These numbers indicate the degree of the chord.

The horizontal lines represent frets.

The "x" indicates that the string is to be muted or not played at all.

This symbol indicates that you are to barre that finger flat across the strings on the same fret.

When a chord is not to be played in open position, a fret marker will indicate where on the neck it is to be played.

CHORD CONSTRUCTION

This section is intended to provide a basic knowledge of chords, how to build them, and how to use them. Some of you may already know this; if so, skip ahead! If not, read on and learn how to impress your friends who don't know.

TRIADS

A chord is simply a collection of notes deliberately arranged in a harmonious (or sometimes non-harmonious) fashion. The most common type of chord is called a triad. The name triad is telling of the number of notes in the chord—three. Triads can be one of four different qualities: major, minor, augmented, or diminished. Below, we find what's known as a C Major triad:

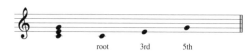

The words "root," "third," and "fifth" below the notes on the staff indicate how each note is functioning within the chord. A root note is the foundation of the chord and the note after which the chord will be named.

INTERVALS

The other two notes in our C triad (the 3rd and the 5th) are responsible for the quality of the chord. The notes C and E are an interval (or distance) of a major 3rd apart. Intervals are comprised of two components: a number and a quality.

We can determine that C to E is a 3rd by simply counting through the musical alphabet. Starting from C: C is one, D is two, and E is three. (The word "root" is many times used interchangeably with the number "1." For all practical purposes, they mean the same thing.) From C to G is a 5th, and we can confirm this by again counting up from C: C(1)–D(2)–E(3)–F(4)–G(5).

Determining the quality of an interval is not quite as easy as the number, but it's not too difficult. It will require a bit of memorization, but it's very logical. Below we'll find all twelve of the notes in the chromatic scale and their intervals measured from a C root note:

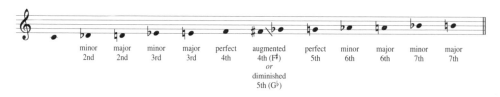

This example tells us a great deal about intervals. We can see a few formulas here at work. The first thing we should notice is that a minor interval is always one half step smaller than a major interval. C to E is a major 3rd, whereas C to E♭ is a minor 3rd. C to A is a major 6th, whereas C to A♭ is a minor 6th, etc. The next thing we should notice is how 4ths and 5ths work. We can see that an augmented interval is always one half step greater than a perfect one, and a diminished interval is always one half step smaller.

Any triad of one of the four above-mentioned qualities will contain a root, 3rd, and 5th. Other types of triads you may encounter include 6 chords, sus4 chords, and sus2 chords. Theses chords are the product of (in the case of sus4 and sus2 chords) replacing the 3rd with another note or (in the case of 6 chords) replacing the 5th (or sometimes adding to it) with another note.

Below are several different qualities of triads, which will allow us to examine these intervals at work and note how they affect the names of these chords:

The symbol ° stands for diminised, while the symbol + stands for augmented.

* Note that the 5th tone may or may not be present in a 6 chord.

7TH CHORDS

Beyond the triad, we'll encounter many more chords, most commonly 7th chords. These chords will not only contain the root, 3rd, and 5th, but also the 7th. Below are a few common 7th chords. (Note that the 7th interval can be major or minor independently of the 3rd, thus affecting the name of the chord.)

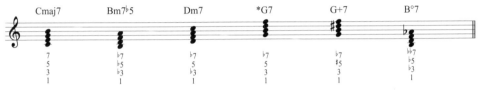

* Note that the G7 chord contains a major 3rd and a minor 7th. This type of chord is referred to as a "dominant 7th."

EXTENSIONS

Finally, beyond 7th chords, we have extensions. The concept of extensions is a bit complicated and will only be touched upon here, as it requires more extensive study than is possible within the scope of this book. Basically, extended chords continue the process of stacking notes onto a triad that we began with the 7th chord. Instead of only adding the 7th to the chord, however, in a 9th chord we'll add the 7th and the 9th. In an 11th chord, we'll add the 7th, 9th, and 11th to our triad, etc. Now, here's the catch: not all of these notes need to be present in order for a chord to be an extension. The general rule is, if the 7th is present, then notes other than the root, 3rd, and 5th are extensions and therefore numbered an octave higher (9, 11, 13). The C13 chord below demonstrates this concept:

Note that there is no 5th (G) present in this chord, but the presence of the 7th (B♭) tells us that this chord is called C13, rather than some kind of C6 chord.

INVERSIONS

Since the banjo only has four strings (commonly used in chordal playing), chords will often be voiced in *inversion*. A chord is inverted when a note other than the root is in the bass. In a triad, which contains three different notes, there are three basic possibilities for the vertical organization of the notes: root position, first inversion, and second inversion. Chords in root position contain the root of the chord in the bass; in other words, they are not inversions. A first inversion chord, however, contains the 3rd in the bass, while a second inversion chord contains the 5th in the bass. This is demonstrated below:

In a seventh chord or an extended chord, which contains four different notes, we have another inversion possibility. In addition to the first and second inversions, we can also have a third inversion, which places the 7th of the chord in the bass.

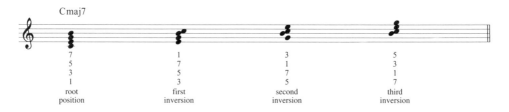

Occasionally, extended chords will feature an extension tone (9th, 11th, or 13th) in the bass. While these chords are inversions as well, they aren't typically numbered as with the triads and seventh chords. For instance, the chord below would most likely be called "a D9 with E in the bass" or "a D9 with the 9th in the bass."

Again, this section is intended to be a basic tutorial on the concept of chord construction and chord theory. If you're interested in furthering your knowledge on this subject (and I recommend it), I suggest you take a look at some of the many books dedicated to this subject.

CHORD QUALITIES

Below is a list of the thirty different chord qualities presented in this book, their abbreviations, and their formulas:

CHORD TYPE	ABBREVIATION	FORMULA
Major	C	1–3–5
Minor	Cm	1–♭3–5
Augmented	C+	1–3–♯5
Diminished	C°	1–♭3–♭5
Fifth (Power Chord)	C5	1–5
Added Ninth	Cadd9	1–3–5–9
Minor Added Ninth	Cm(add9)	1–♭3–5–9
Suspended Fourth	Csus4	1–4–5
Suspended Second	Csus2	1–2–5
Sixth	C6	1–3–5–6
Minor Sixth	Cm6	1–♭3–5–6
Major Seventh	Cmaj7	1–3–5–7
Major Seventh, Sharp Fifth	Cmaj7♯5	1–3–♯5–7
Major Seventh, Flat Fifth	Cmaj7♭5	1–3–♭5–7
Major Ninth	Cmaj9	1–3–5–7–9
Major Thirteenth	Cmaj13	1–3–5–7–9–13
Minor Seventh	Cm7	1–♭3–5–♭7
Minor, Major Seventh	Cm(maj7)	1–♭3–5–7
Minor Seventh, Flat Fifth	Cm7♭5	1–♭3–♭5–♭7
Minor Ninth	Cm9	1–♭3–5–♭7–9
Minor Eleventh	Cm11	1–♭3–5–♭7–9–11
Seventh	C7	1–3–5–♭7
Seventh, Suspended Fourth	C7sus4	1–4–5–♭7
Augmented Seventh	C+7	1–3–♯5–♭7
Seventh, Flat Fifth	C7♭5	1–3–♭5–♭7
Ninth	C9	1–3–5–♭7–9
Seventh, Sharp Ninth	C7♯9	1–3–5–♭7–♯9
Seventh, Flat Ninth	C7♭9	1–3–5–♭7–♭9
Eleventh	C11	1–3–5–♭7–9–11*
Thirteenth	C13	1–3–5–♭7–9–11–13 **
Diminished Seventh	C°7	1–♭3–♭5–♭♭7

* The 3rd is sometimes omitted from an eleventh chord.
** The 11th is sometimes omitted from a thirteenth chord.

NOTES ON TRANSPOSING

This book is designed to provide many unique voicings by taking advantage of open strings in certain keys. However, the use of a capo is extremely common in banjo playing and is a simple way to play in another key while using the same chord shapes. This is particularly useful when playing with other musicians. For example, let's say you're used to playing a certain tune that's in G major with open G tuning, but the band you're playing with likes to play it in A major. Simply place a capo on the second fret, and your open G tuning essentially becomes an open A tuning. You can now play all the same shapes that you did in open G, but they will now sound a whole step higher in A.

Alternatively, it's also common to simply retune the banjo to the new key. In the previous example, you could raise each string of your banjo by a whole step, creating an open A tuning. Generally speaking, capos work fine when you're playing mostly chord shapes and not straying too far from open position. If you're playing a lot of melodies up high on the neck, however, it's probably better to tune up. This way you won't have to worry about remembering to play everything two frets higher.

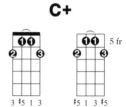

C

C

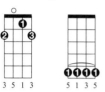

3 5 1 3   5 1 3 5

Cm

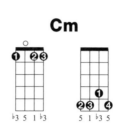

♭3 5 1 ♭3   5 1 ♭3 5

C+

5 fr

3 ♯5 1 3   ♯5 1 3 ♯5

C°

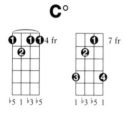

4 fr   7 fr

♭5 1 ♭3 ♭5   1 ♭3 ♭5 1

C5

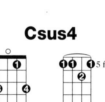

x   x

5 fr   8 fr

5 1 5   1   5 1

Cadd9

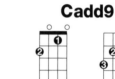

8 fr

3 5 1 9   1 3 5 9

Cm(add9)

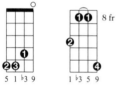

8 fr

5 1 ♭3 9   1 ♭3 5 9

Csus4

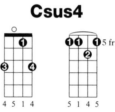

5 fr

4 5 1 4   5 1 4 5

Csus2

2 5 1 2   5 1 2 5

C6

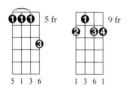

5 fr   9 fr

5 1 3 6   1 3 6 1

Cm6

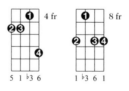

4 fr   8 fr

5 1 ♭3 6   1 ♭3 6 1

Cmaj7

8 fr

5 1 7 3   1 3 5 7

Cmaj7♯5

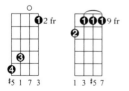

2 fr   9 fr

♯5 1 7 3   1 3 ♯5 7

Cmaj7♭5

7 fr

♭5 1 7 3   1 3 ♭5 7

Cmaj9

9 fr

3 7 1 9   1 3 7 9

Open G

C

Cmaj13
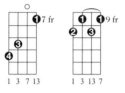

Cm7

Cm(maj7)
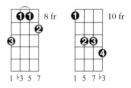

Cm7♭5
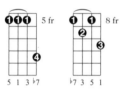

Cm9
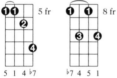

Cm11
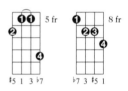

C7

C7sus4

C+7
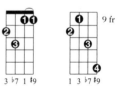

C7♭5
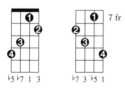

C9

C7#9

C11
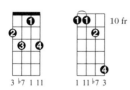

C13
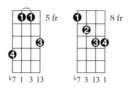

C°7
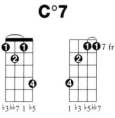

Cm7
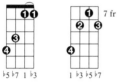

D♭

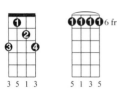

3 5 1 3   5 1 3 5

D♭m

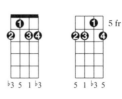

♭3 5 1 ♭3   5 1 ♭3 5

D♭+

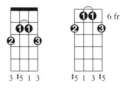

3 ♯5 1 3   ♯5 1 3 ♯5

D♭°

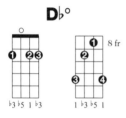

♭3 ♭5 1 ♭3   1 ♭3 ♭5 1

D♭5

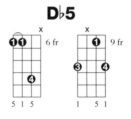

5 1 5   1 5 1

D♭add9

3 5 1 9   1 3 5 9

D♭m(add9)

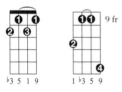

♭3 5 1 9   1 ♭3 5 9

D♭sus4

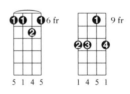

5 1 4 5   1 4 5 1

D♭sus2

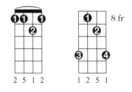

2 5 1 2   1 2 5 1

D♭6

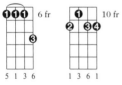

5 1 3 6   1 3 6 1

D♭m6

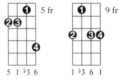

5 1 ♭3 6   1 ♭3 6 1

D♭maj7

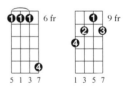

5 1 3 7   1 3 5 7

D♭maj7♯5

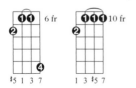

♯5 1 3 7   1 3 ♯5 7

D♭maj7♭5

♭5 7 1 3   1 3 ♭5 7

D♭maj9

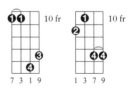

7 3 1 9   1 3 7 9

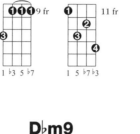

D♭maj13
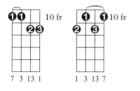

D♭m7

D♭m(maj7)
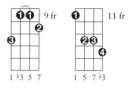

D♭m7♭5
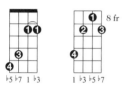

D♭m9

D♭m11
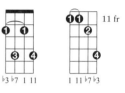

D♭7
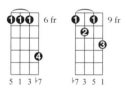

D♭7sus4

D♭+7
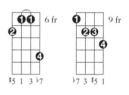

D♭7♭5
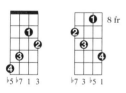

D♭9
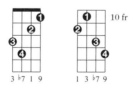

D♭7♯9
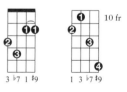

D♭11
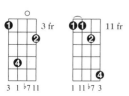

D♭13
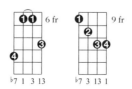

D♭°7
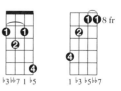

11

D

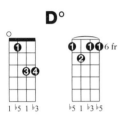

1 5 1 3   5 1 3 5

Dm

1 5 1 ♭3   5 1 ♭3 5

D+

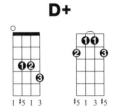

1 ♯5 1 3   ♯5 1 3 ♯5

D°

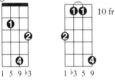

1 ♭5 1 ♭3   ♭5 1 ♭3 5

D5

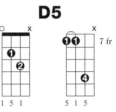 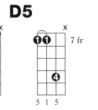

1 5 1   5 1 5

Dadd9

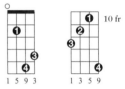

1 5 9 3   1 3 5 9

Dm(add9)

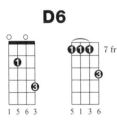

1 5 9 ♭3   1 ♭3 5 9

Dsus4

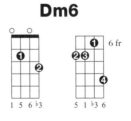

1 5 1 4   5 1 4 5

Dsus2

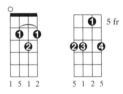

1 5 1 2   5 1 2 5

D6

1 5 6 3   5 1 3 6

Dm6

1 5 6 ♭3   5 1 ♭3 6

Dmaj7

1 5 7 3   1 3 5 7

Dmaj7♯5

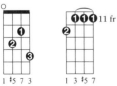

1 ♯5 7 3   1 3 ♯5 7

Dmaj7♭5

1 ♭5 7 3   1 3 ♭5 7

Dmaj9

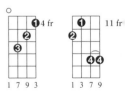

1 7 9 3   1 3 7 9

D

Dmaj13
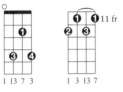
1 13 7 3   1 3 13 7   11 fr

Dm7
1 5 ♭7 ♭3   1 ♭3 5 ♭7   10 fr

Dm(maj7)
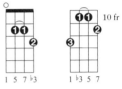
1 5 7 ♭3   1 ♭3 5 7   10 fr

Dm7♭5
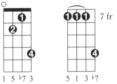
1 ♭5 ♭7 ♭3   ♭5 ♭7 1 ♭3   3 fr

Dm9
1 ♭7 9 ♭3   1 ♭3 ♭7 9   10 fr

Dm11
1 11 ♭7 ♭3   ♭3 ♭7 1 11

D7
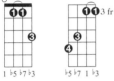
1 5 ♭7 3   5 1 3 ♭7   7 fr

D7sus4
1 ♭7 4 5   5 fr   5 1 4 ♭7   7 fr

D+7
1 ♯5 ♭7 3   ♯5 1 3 ♭7   7 fr

D7♭5
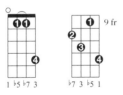
1 ♭5 ♭7 3   ♭7 3 ♭5 1   9 fr

D9
1 ♭7 9 3   1 3 ♭7 9   11 fr

D7♯9
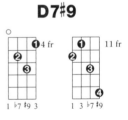
1 ♭7 ♯9 3   4 fr   1 3 ♭7 ♯9   11 fr

D11
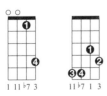
1 11 ♭7 3   11 ♭7 1 3

D13
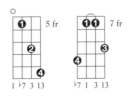
1 ♭7 3 13   5 fr   ♭7 1 3 13   7 fr

D°7
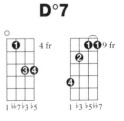
1 ♭♭7 ♭3 ♭5   4 fr   1 ♭3 ♭5 ♭♭7   9 fr

Eb

3 5 1 3   5 1 3 5

Ebm

b3 5 1 b3   5 1 b3 5

Eb+
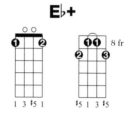
1 3 #5 1   #5 1 3 #5

Eb°

1 b5 1 b3   b5 1 b3 b5

Eb5
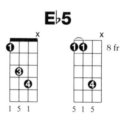
1 5 1   5 1 5

Ebadd9
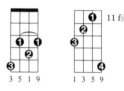
3 5 1 9   1 3 5 9

Ebm(add9)
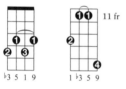
b3 5 1 9   1 b3 5 9

Ebsus4
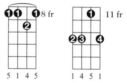
5 1 4 5   1 4 5 1

Ebsus2
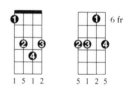
1 5 1 2   5 1 2 5

Eb6
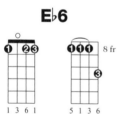
1 3 6 1   5 1 3 6

Ebm6
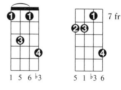
1 5 6 b3   5 1 b3 6

Ebmaj7
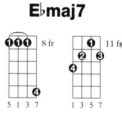
5 1 3 7   1 3 5 7

Ebmaj7#5
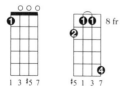
1 3 #5 7   #5 1 3 7

Ebmaj7b5
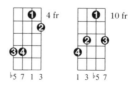
b5 7 1 3   1 3 b5 7

Ebmaj9
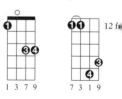
1 3 7 9   7 3 1 9

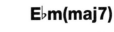

E♭maj13
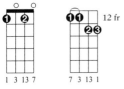
12 fr
1 3 13 7   7 3 13 1

E♭m7
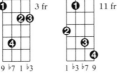
11 fr
1 5 ♭7 ♭3   1 ♭3 5 ♭7

E♭m(maj7)
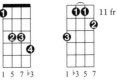
11 fr
1 5 7 ♭3   1 ♭3 5 7

E♭m7♭5
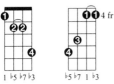
4 fr
1 ♭5 ♭7 ♭3   ♭5 ♭7 1 ♭3

E♭m9
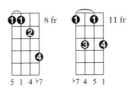
3 fr   11 fr
9 ♭7 1 ♭3   1 ♭3 ♭7 9

E♭m11
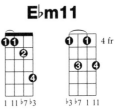
4 fr
1 11 ♭7 ♭3   ♭3 ♭7 1 11

E♭7
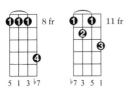
8 fr   11 fr
5 1 3 ♭7   ♭7 3 5 1

E♭7sus4
8 fr   11 fr
5 1 4 ♭7   ♭7 4 5 1

E♭+7
8 fr   11 fr
♯5 1 3 ♭7   ♭7 3 ♯5 1

E♭7♭5
4 fr   10 fr
♭5 ♭7 1 3   ♭7 3 ♭5 1

E♭9
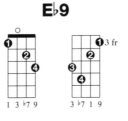
3 fr
1 3 ♭7 9   3 ♭7 1 9

E♭7♯9
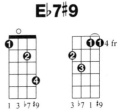
4 fr
1 3 ♭7 ♯9   3 ♭7 1 ♯9

E♭11
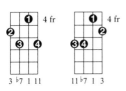
4 fr   4 fr
3 ♭7 1 11   11 ♭7 1 3

E♭13
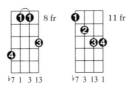
8 fr   11 fr
♭7 1 3 13   ♭7 3 13 1

E♭°7
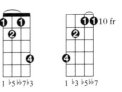
10 fr
1 ♭5 ♭♭7 ♭3   1 ♭3 ♭5 ♭♭7

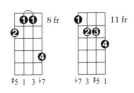
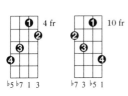

E

E
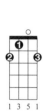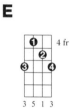

1 3 5 1   3 5 1 3   4 fr

Em
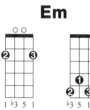

1 ♭3 5 1   ♭3 5 1 ♭3

E+
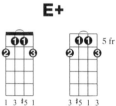

1 3 ♯5 1   3 ♯5 1 3   5 fr

E°
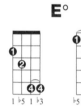

1 ♭5 1 ♭3   ♭5 1 ♭3 ♭5   8 fr

E5
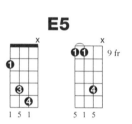

1 5 1   5 1 5   9 fr

Eadd9
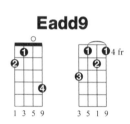

1 3 5 9   3 5 1 9   4 fr

Em(add9)
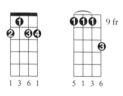

1 ♭3 5 9   ♭3 5 1 9

Esus4
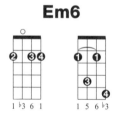

1 4 5 1   5 1 4 5   9 fr

Esus2
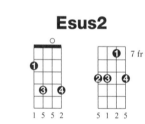

1 5 5 2   5 1 2 5   7 fr

E6

1 3 6 1   5 1 3 6   9 fr

Em6
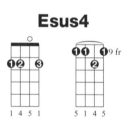

1 ♭3 6 1   1 5 6 ♭3

Emaj7

1 3 5 7   5 1 3 7   9 fr

Emaj7♯5
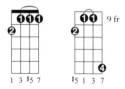

1 3 ♯5 7   ♯5 1 3 7   9 fr

Emaj7♭5
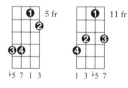

♭5 7 1 3   1 3 ♭5 7   5 fr   11 fr

Emaj9
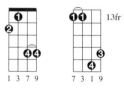

1 3 7 9   7 3 1 9   13fr

E

Emaj13

1 3 13 7   7 3 13 1

Em7

1 ♭3 5 ♭7   1 5 ♭7 ♭3

Em(maj7)
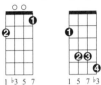

1 ♭3 5 7   1 5 7 ♭3

Em7♭5
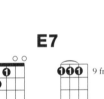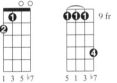

5 fr

1 ♭5 ♭7 ♭3   ♭5 ♭7 1 ♭3

Em9
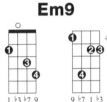

4 fr

1 ♭3 ♭7 9   9 ♭7 1 ♭3

Em11
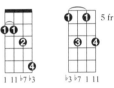

5 fr

1 11 ♭7 ♭3   ♭3 ♭7 1 11

E7
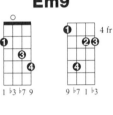

9 fr

1 3 5 ♭7   5 1 3 ♭7

E7sus4
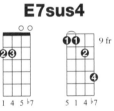

9 fr

1 4 5 ♭7   5 1 4 ♭7

E+7
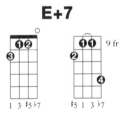

9 fr

1 3 ♯5 ♭7   ♯5 1 3 ♭7

E7♭5
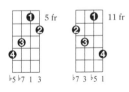

5 fr   11 fr

♭5 ♭7 1 3   ♭7 3 ♭5 1

E9
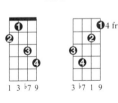

4 fr

1 3 ♭7 9   3 ♭7 1 9

E7♯9
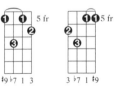

5 fr   5 fr

♯9 ♭7 1 3   3 ♭7 1 ♯9

E11
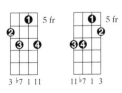

5 fr   5 fr

3 ♭7 1 11   11 ♭7 1 3

E13
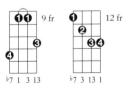

9 fr   12 fr

♭7 1 3 13   ♭7 3 13 1

E°7
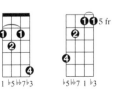

5 fr

1 ♭5 ♭♭7 ♭3   ♭5 ♭♭7 1 ♭3

17

F

F

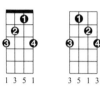

1 3 5 1   3 5 1 3

Fm

1 ♭3 5 1   ♭3 5 1 ♭3

F+

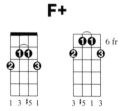

1 3 ♯5 1   3 ♯5 1 3

F°

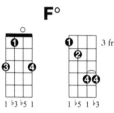

1 ♭3 ♭5 1   1 ♭5 1 ♭3

F5

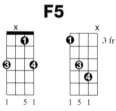

1   5 1   1 5 1

Fadd9

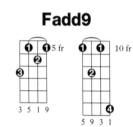

3 5 1 9   5 9 3 1

Fm(add9)

9 5 1 ♭3   ♭3 5 1 9

Fsus4

1 4 5 1   5 1 4 5

Fsus2

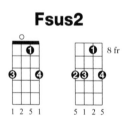

1 2 5 1   5 1 2 5

F6

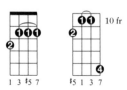

1 3 5 6   1 3 6 1

Fm6

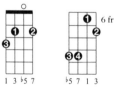

1 ♭3 5 6   1 ♭3 6 1

Fmaj7

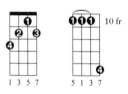

1 3 5 7   5 1 3 7

Fmaj7♯5

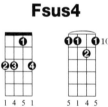

1 3 ♯5 7   ♯5 1 3 7

Fmaj7♭5

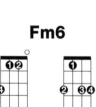

1 3 ♭5 7   ♭5 7 1 3

Fmaj9

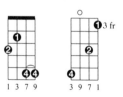

1 3 7 9   3 9 7 1

Fmaj13

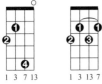

1 3 7 13   1 3 13 7

Fm7

1 ♭3 5 ♭7   1 5 ♭7 ♭3

3 fr

Fm(maj7)

1 ♭3 5 7   1 5 7 ♭3

3 fr

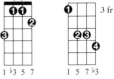

Fm7♭5

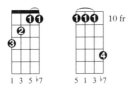

1 ♭3 ♭5 ♭7   1 ♭5 ♭7 ♭3

3 fr

Fm9

1 ♭3 ♭7 9   ♭3 ♭7 1 9

5 fr

Fm11

1 11 ♭7 ♭3   ♭3 ♭7 1 11

3 fr   6 fr

F7

1 3 5 ♭7   5 1 3 ♭7

10 fr

F7sus4

1 4 5 ♭7   5 1 4 ♭7

10 fr

F+7

1 3 ♯5 ♭7   ♯5 1 3 ♭7

10 fr

F7♭5

1 3 ♭5 ♭7   ♭5 ♭7 1 3

6 fr

F9

1 3 ♭7 9   3 ♭7 1 9

5 fr

F7♯9

♯9 ♭7 1 3   3 ♭7 1 ♯9

6 fr   6 fr

F11

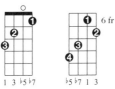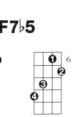

3 ♭7 1 11   11 ♭7 1 3

6 fr   6 fr

F13

♭7 3 13 1   1 3 ♭7 13

F°7

1 ♭3 ♭5 ♭♭7   1 ♭5 ♭♭7 ♭3

3 fr

F#

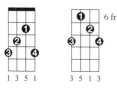

1 3 5 1   3 5 1 3   6 fr

F#m

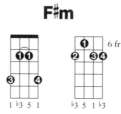

1 ♭3 5 1   ♭3 5 1 ♭3   6 fr

F#+

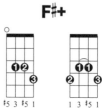

♯5 3 ♯5 1   1 3 ♯5 1

F#°

1 ♭5 1 ♭3   4 fr   ♭5 1 ♭3 ♭5   10 fr

F#5

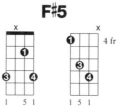

1   5 1   1 5 1   4 fr

F#add9

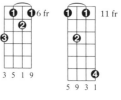

3 5 1 9   6 fr   5 9 3 1   11 fr

F#m(add9)

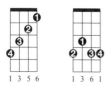

9 5 1 ♭3   6 fr   ♭3 5 1 9   6 fr

F#sus4

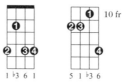

1 4 5 1   5 1 4 5   11 fr

F#sus2

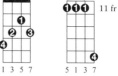

1 5 1 2   4 fr   5 1 2 5   9 fr

F#6

1 3 5 6   1 3 6 1

F#m6

1 ♭3 6 1   5 1 ♭3 6   10 fr

F#maj7

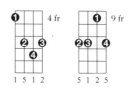

1 3 5 7   5 1 3 7   11 fr

F#maj7#5

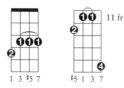

1 3 ♯5 7   ♯5 1 3 7   11 fr

F#maj7♭5

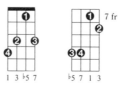

1 3 ♭5 7   ♭5 7 1 3   7 fr

F#maj9

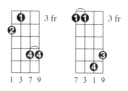

1 3 7 9   3 fr   7 3 1 9   3 fr

F#

F#maj13
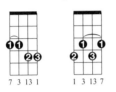
7 3 13 1   1 3 13 7

F#m7
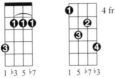

4 fr
1 ♭3 5 ♭7   1 5 ♭7 ♭3

F#m(maj7)
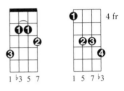
4 fr
1 ♭3 5 7   1 5 7 ♭3

F#m7♭5
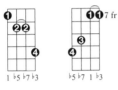
1 ♭5 ♭7 ♭3   ♭5 ♭7 1 ♭3   7 fr

F#m9
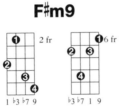
2 fr   6 fr
1 ♭3 ♭7 9   ♭3 ♭7 1 9

F#m11
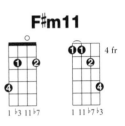
4 fr
1 ♭3 11 ♭7   1 11 ♭7 ♭3

F#7
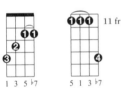
1 3 5 ♭7   5 1 3 ♭7   11 fr

F#7sus4
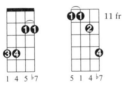
11 fr
1 4 5 ♭7   5 1 4 ♭7

F#+7
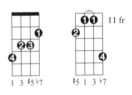
11 fr
1 3 #5 ♭7   #5 1 3 ♭7

F#7♭5

7 fr
1 3 ♭5 ♭7   ♭5 ♭7 1 3

F#9
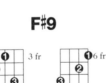
3 fr   6 fr
1 3 ♭7 9   3 ♭7 1 9

F#7#9
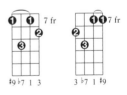
7 fr   7 fr
#9 ♭7 1 3   3 ♭7 1 #9

F#11
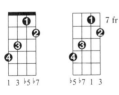
1 3 11 ♭7   3 ♭7 1 11   7 fr

F#13
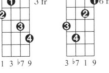

11 fr
♭7 3 13 1   ♭7 1 3 13

F#°7
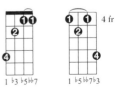
4 fr
1 ♭3 ♭5 ♭♭7   1 ♭5 ♭♭7 ♭3

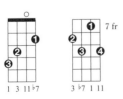

G

5 1 3 5   1 3 5 1

Gm

7 fr

1 ♭3 5 1   ♭3 5 1 ♭3

G+

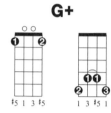

♯5 1 3 ♯5   1 3 ♯5 1

G°

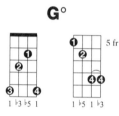

5 fr

1 ♭3 ♭5 1   1 ♭5 1 ♭3

G5

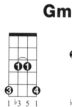

5 fr

x

5 1 5 1   1 5 1

Gadd9

7 fr

5 9 3 1   3 5 1 9

Gm(add9)

7 fr   7 fr

9 5 1 ♭3   ♭3 5 1 9

Gsus4

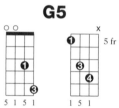

5 1 4 5   1 4 5 1

Gsus2

5 fr

5 2 5 1   1 5 1 2

G6

5 1 3 6   1 3 6 1

Gm6

6 ♭3 5 1   1 ♭3 6 1

Gmaj7

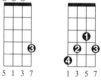

5 1 3 7   1 3 5 7

Gmaj7♯5

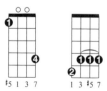

♯5 1 3 7   1 3 ♯5 7

Gmaj7♭5

8 fr

1 3 ♭5 7   ♭5 7 1 3

Gmaj9

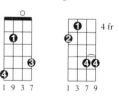

4 fr

1 9 3 7   1 3 7 9

G

Gmaj13

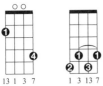
13 1 3 7   1 3 13 7

Gm7
5 fr
1 ♭3 5 ♭7   1 5 ♭7 ♭3

Gm(maj7)

5 fr
1 ♭3 5 7   1 5 7 ♭3

Gm7♭5
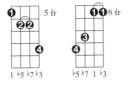
5 fr   8 fr
1 ♭5 ♭7 ♭3   ♭5 ♭7 1 ♭3

Gm9

3 fr   6 fr
1 ♭3 ♭7 9   ♭3 1 ♭7 9

Gm11
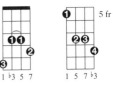
5 fr   8 fr
1 11 ♭7 ♭3   ♭3 ♭7 1 11

G7
5 1 3 ♭7   1 3 5 ♭7

G7sus4
5 1 4 ♭7   1 4 5 ♭7

G+7
♯5 1 3 ♭7   1 3 ♯5 ♭7

G7♭5
♭7 3 ♭5 1   1 3 ♭5 ♭7

G9

4 fr
1 9 3 ♭7   1 3 ♭7 9

G7♯9

4 fr
♭7 ♯9 3 1   1 3 ♭7 ♯9

G11
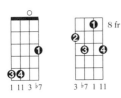
8 fr
1 11 3 ♭7   3 ♭7 1 11

G13
♭7 1 3 13   ♭7 3 13 1

G°7
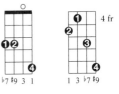
5 fr
1 ♭3 ♭5 ♭♭7   1 ♭5 ♭♭7 ♭3

Ab

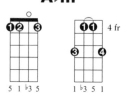

5 1 3 5   1 3 5 1   4 fr

Abm

5 1 b3 5   1 b3 5 1   4 fr

Ab+

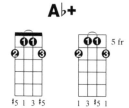

#5 1 3 #5   1 3 #5 1   5 fr

Ab°

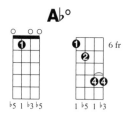

b5 1 b3 b5   1 b5 1 b3   6 fr

Ab5

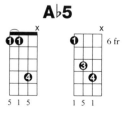

5 1 5   1 5 1   6 fr

Abadd9

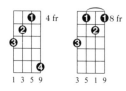

1 3 5 9   4 fr   3 5 1 9   8 fr

Abm(add9)

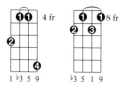

1 b3 5 9   4 fr   b3 5 1 9   8 fr

Absus4

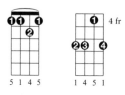

5 1 4 5   1 4 5 1   4 fr

Absus2

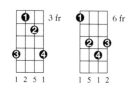

1 2 5 1   3 fr   1 5 1 2   6 fr

Ab6

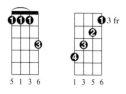

5 1 3 6   1 3 5 6   3 fr

Abm6

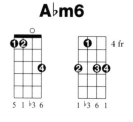

5 1 b3 6   1 b3 6 1   4 fr

Abmaj7

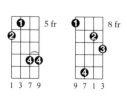

7 3 5 1   4 fr   1 3 5 7   4 fr

Abmaj7#5

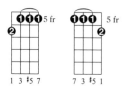

1 3 #5 7   5 fr   7 3 #5 1   5 fr

Abmaj7b5

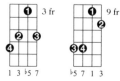

1 3 b5 7   3 fr   b5 7 1 3   9 fr

Abmaj9

1 3 7 9   5 fr   9 7 1 3   8 fr

Abmaj13

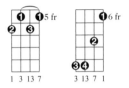

Abm7

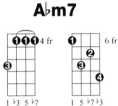

Abm(maj7)

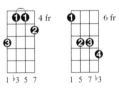

Abm7b5

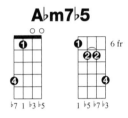

Abm9

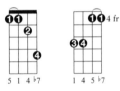

Abm11

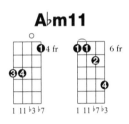

Ab7

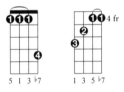

Ab7sus4

Ab+7

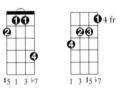

Ab7b5

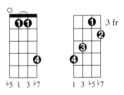

Ab9

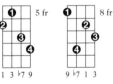

Ab7#9

Ab11

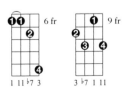

Ab13

Ab°7

25

A

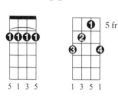

Am

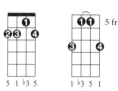

A+

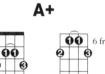
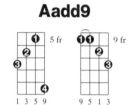

A°

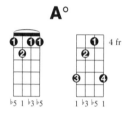

A5

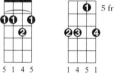

Aadd9

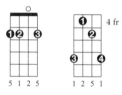

Am(add9)

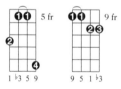

Asus4

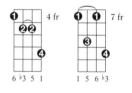

Asus2

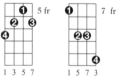

A6

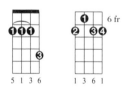

Am6

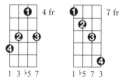

Amaj7

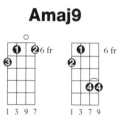

Amaj7#5

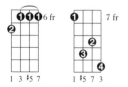

Amaj7♭5

Amaj9

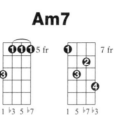

A

Amaj13

Am7

Am(maj7)

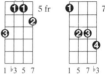

Am7♭5

Am9

Am11

A7

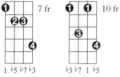

A7sus4

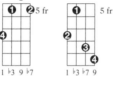

A+7

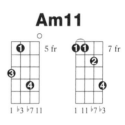

A7♭5

A9

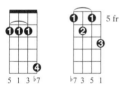

A7#9

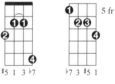

A11

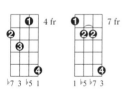

A13

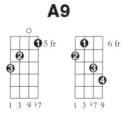

A°7

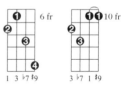

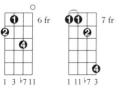

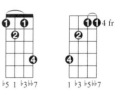

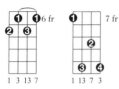

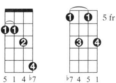

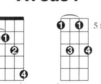

B♭

B♭

```
5 1 3 5        1 3 5 1
```
6 fr

B♭m

```
5 1 ♭3 5       1 ♭3 5 1
```
6 fr

B♭+

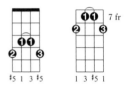

```
♯5 1 3 ♯5      1 3 ♯5 1
```
7 fr

B♭°

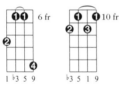

```
♭5 1 ♭3 ♭5     1 ♭3 ♭5 1
```
5 fr

B♭5

```
5 1 5          1   5 1
```
3 fr   6 fr

B♭add9

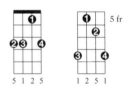

```
5 1 9 3        1 3 5 9
```
6 fr

B♭m(add9)

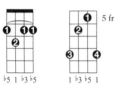

```
1 ♭3 5 9       ♭3 5 1 9
```
6 fr   10 fr

B♭sus4

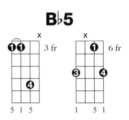

```
5 1 4 5        1 4 5 1
```
6 fr

B♭sus2

```
5 1 2 5        1 2 5 1
```
5 fr

B♭6

```
5 1 3 6        3 1 5 6
```
3 fr

B♭m6

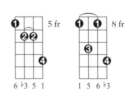

```
6 ♭3 5 1       1 5 6 ♭3
```
5 fr   8 fr

B♭maj7

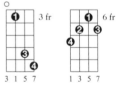

```
3 1 5 7        1 3 5 7
```
3 fr   6 fr

B♭maj7♯5

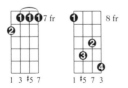

```
1 3 ♯5 7       1 ♯5 7 3
```
7 fr   8 fr

B♭maj7♭5

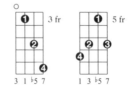

```
3 1 ♭5 7       1 3 ♭5 7
```
3 fr   5 fr

B♭maj9

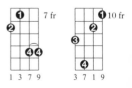

```
1 3 7 9        3 7 1 9
```
7 fr   10 fr

B♭

B♭maj13

B♭m7

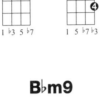

B♭m(maj7)

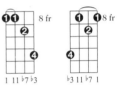

B♭m7♭5

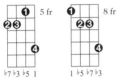

B♭m9

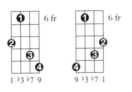

B♭m11

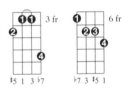

B♭7

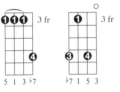

B♭7sus4

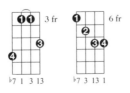

B♭+7

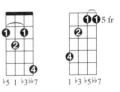

B♭7♭5

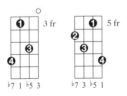

B♭9

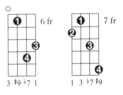

B♭7#9

B♭11

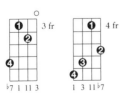

B♭13

B♭°7

B

B

Bm
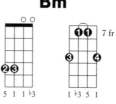

B+
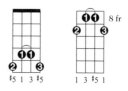

B°
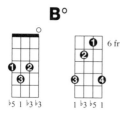

B5
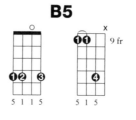

Badd9
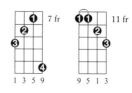

Bm(add9)
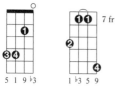

Bsus4
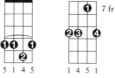

Bsus2
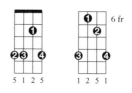

B6
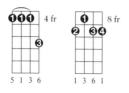

Bm6
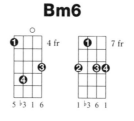

Bmaj7
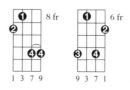

Bmaj7#5
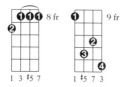

Bmaj7♭5
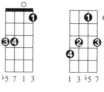

Bmaj9

B

Bmaj13
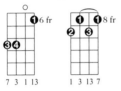

Bm7
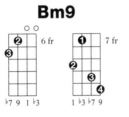

Bm(maj7)
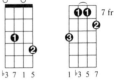

Bm7♭5
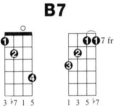

Bm9
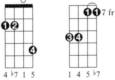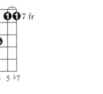

Bm11
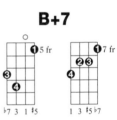

B7
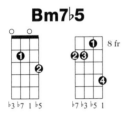

B7sus4
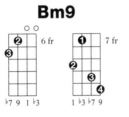

B+7
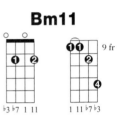

B7♭5

B9

B7#9

B11
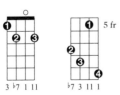

B13
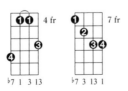

B°7
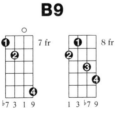

C

C

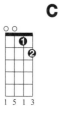

1 5 1 3   3 1 3 5

Cm

1 5 1 ♭3   ♭3 1 ♭3 5

C+

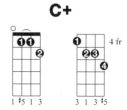

1 ♯5 1 3   3 1 3 ♯5   4 fr

C°

1 1 ♭3 ♭5   ♭3 1 ♭3 ♭5

C5

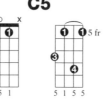

1 5 1   5 1 5 5   5 fr

Cadd9

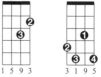

1 5 9 3   3 1 9 5

Cm(add9)

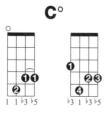

1 5 9 ♭3   ♭3 1 9 5

Csus4

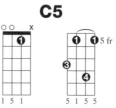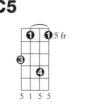

1 5 1 4   4 1 4 5   5 fr

Csus2

1 5 1 2   5 2 5 1   7 fr

C6

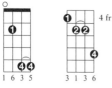

1 6 3 5   3 1 3 6   4 fr

Cm6

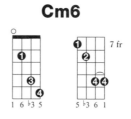

1 6 ♭3 5   5 ♭3 6 1   7 fr

Cmaj7

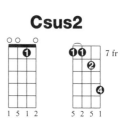

1 5 7 3   5 1 3 7   5 fr

Cmaj7♯5

1 ♯5 7 3   ♯5 1 3 7   5 fr

Cmaj7♭5

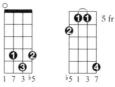

1 7 3 ♭5   ♭5 1 3 7   5 fr

Cmaj9

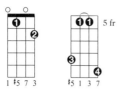

1 7 3 9   1 3 7 9   9 fr

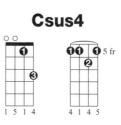

C

Cmaj13

Cm7

Cm(maj7)

Cm7♭5
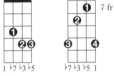

Cm9

Cm11

C7

C7sus4

C+7

C7♭5

C9

C7♯9

C11
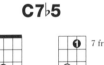

C13

C°7

Db

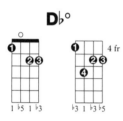
1 5 1 3   3 1 3 5   5 fr

Dbm

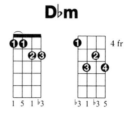
1 5 1 b3   b3 1 b3 5   4 fr

Db+

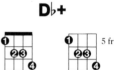
1 #5 1 3   3 1 3 #5   5 fr

Db°

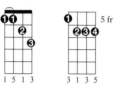
1 b5 1 b3   b3 1 b3 b5   4 fr

Db5

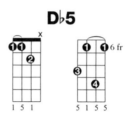
1 5 1   5 1 5 5   6 fr

Dbadd9

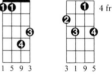
1 5 9 3   3 1 9 5   4 fr

Dbm(add9)

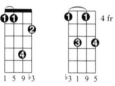
1 5 9 b3   b3 1 9 5   4 fr

Dbsus4

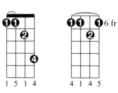
1 5 1 4   4 1 4 5   6 fr

Dbsus2

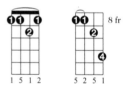
1 5 1 2   5 2 5 1   8 fr

Db6

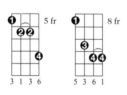
3 1 3 6   5 3 6 1   5 fr   8 fr

Dbm6

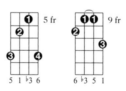
5 1 b3 6   6 b3 5 1   5 fr   9 fr

Dbmaj7

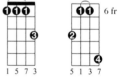
1 5 7 3   5 1 3 7   6 fr

Dbmaj7#5

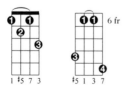
1 #5 7 3   #5 1 3 7   6 fr

Dbmaj7b5

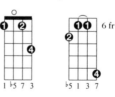
1 b5 7 3   b5 1 3 7   6 fr

Dbmaj9

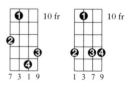
7 3 1 9   1 3 7 9   10 fr   10 fr

Db

Dbmaj13

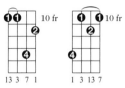

10 fr

13 3 7 1   1 3 13 7

Dbm7

O

9 fr

1 5 b7 3   b7 b3 5 1

Dbm(maj7)

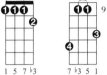

9 fr

1 5 7 b3   7 b3 5 1

Dbm7b5

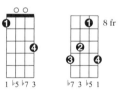

8 fr

1 b5 b7 b3   b7 b3 b5 1

Dbm9

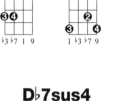

9 fr

b3 b7 1 9   1 b3 b7 9

Dbm11

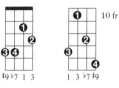

11 fr

b3 b7 1 11   b7 11 1 b3

Db7

O

9 fr

1 5 b7 3   b7 3 5 1

Db7sus4

O

6 fr   9 fr

4 1 b7 5   b7 4 5 1

Db+7

O

10 fr

1 #5 b7 3   b7 3 #5 1

Db7b5

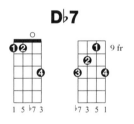

8 fr

1 b5 b7 3   b7 3 b5 1

Db9

10 fr

9 b7 1 3   1 3 b7 9

Db7#9

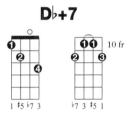

10 fr

#9 b7 1 3   1 3 b7 #9

Db11

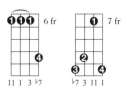

6 fr   7 fr

11 1 3 b7   b7 3 11 1

Db13

O

10 fr

1 13 b7 3   b7 3 13 1

Db°7

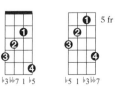

5 fr

b3 bb7 1 b5   b5 1 b3 bb7

D

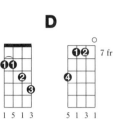

1 5 1 3   5 1 3 1   7 fr

Dm

1 5 1 ♭3   5 1 ♭3 1   6 fr

D+

1 ♯5 1 3   3 1 3 ♯5   6 fr

D°

1 ♭5 1 ♭3   ♭5 1 ♭3 1   6 fr

D5

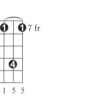

1 5 1 1   5 1 5 5   7 fr

Dadd9

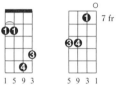

1 5 9 3   5 9 3 1   7 fr

Dm(add9)

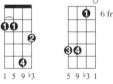

1 5 9 ♭3   5 9 ♭3 1   6 fr

Dsus4

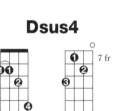

1 5 1 4   5 1 4 1   7 fr

Dsus2

1 5 1 2   5 2 5 1   9 fr

D6

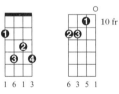

1 6 1 3   6 3 5 1   10 fr

Dm6

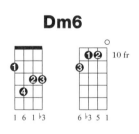

1 6 1 ♭3   6 ♭3 5 1   10 fr

Dmaj7

1 5 7 3   5 1 3 7   7 fr

Dmaj7♯5

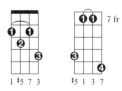

1 ♯5 7 3   ♯5 1 3 7   7 fr

Dmaj7♭5

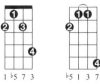

1 ♭5 7 3   ♭5 1 3 7   7 fr

Dmaj9

3 7 9 1   1 3 7 9   5 fr / 11 fr

36

D

Dmaj13

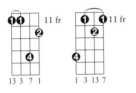

11 fr   11 fr

13 3 7 1   1 3 13 7

Dm7

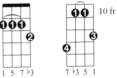

10 fr

1 5 ♭7 3   ♭7 3 5 1

Dm(maj7)

10 fr

1 5 7 ♭3   7 ♭3 5 1

Dm7♭5

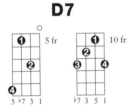

9 fr

1 ♭5 ♭7 3   ♭7 3 ♭5 1

Dm9

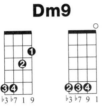

♭3 ♭7 1 9   ♭3 ♭7 9 1

Dm11

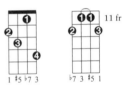

♭7 11 1 ♭3   ♭3 ♭7 1 11

D7

5 fr   10 fr

5 ♭7 3 1   ♭7 3 5 1

D7sus4

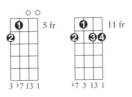

5 fr   10 fr

5 ♭7 4 1   ♭7 4 5 1

D+7

11 fr

1 ♯5 ♭7 3   ♭7 3 ♯5 1

D7♭5

5 fr

1 ♭5 ♭7 3   ♭5 ♭7 3 1

D9

5 fr

1 ♭7 9 3   3 ♭7 9 1

D7♯9

5 fr

♯9 ♭7 1 3   3 ♭7 ♯9 1

D11

7 fr

1 11 ♭7 3   11 1 3 ♭7

D13

5 fr   11 fr

3 ♭7 13 1   ♭7 3 13 1

D°7

3 fr

1 ♭5 ♭♭7 3   ♭3 ♭♭7 1 ♭5

E♭

1 5 1 3   3 1 3 5

E♭m

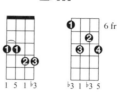

1 5 1 ♭3   ♭3 1 ♭3 5

E♭+

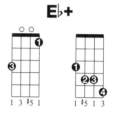

1 3 ♯5 1   1 ♯5 1 3

E♭°

1 ♭5 1 ♭3   ♭3 1 ♭3 ♭5

E♭5

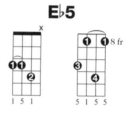

1 5 1   5 1 5 5

E♭add9

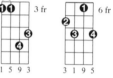

1 5 9 3   3 1 9 5

E♭m(add9)

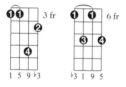

1 5 9 ♭3   ♭3 1 9 5

E♭sus4

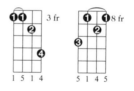

1 5 1 4   5 1 4 5

E♭sus2

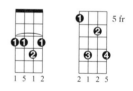

1 5 1 2   2 1 2 5

E♭6

1 6 1 3   5 3 6 1

E♭m6

1 6 1 ♭3   ♭3 6 1 5

E♭maj7

1 5 7 3   5 1 3 7

E♭maj7♯5

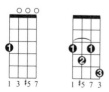

1 3 ♯5 7   1 ♯5 7 3

E♭maj7♭5

1 ♭5 7 3   ♭5 1 3 7

E♭maj9

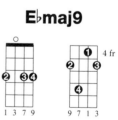

1 3 7 9   9 7 1 3

E♭

E♭maj13

1 3 13 7   13 3 7 1   12 fr

E♭m7

1 5 ♭7 3   ♭7 ♭3 5 1   11 fr

E♭m(maj7)

1 5 7 ♭3   5 1 ♭3 7   7 fr

E♭m7♭5

1 ♭5 ♭7 ♭3   ♭7 ♭3 ♭5 1   10 fr

E♭m9

♭3 ♭7 1 9   3 fr   9 ♭7 1 ♭3   4 fr

E♭m11

♭7 11 1 ♭3   ♭3 ♭7 1 11   4 fr

E♭7

3 ♭7 1 5   4 fr   ♭7 3 5 1   11 fr

E♭7sus4

4 ♭7 1 5   4 fr   ♭7 4 5 1   11 fr

E♭+7

♭7 3 ♯5 1   1 ♯5 ♭7 3

E♭7♭5

1 ♭5 ♭7 3   3 ♭7 1 ♭5   4 fr

E♭9

1 3 ♭7 9   3 fr   1 ♭7 9 3

E♭7♯9

1 3 ♭7 ♯9   4 fr   ♯9 ♭7 1 3

E♭11

11 1 3 ♭7   8 fr   ♭7 3 11 1   9 fr

E♭13

♭7 3 13 1   13 3 ♭7 1   12 fr

E♭°7

1 ♭5 ♭♭7 ♭3   ♭♭7 ♭5 1 ♭3

39

E

E
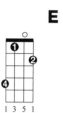

1 3 5 1   1 5 1 3

Em
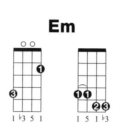

1 ♭3 5 1   1 5 1 ♭3

E+
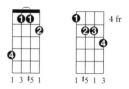

1 3 ♯5 1   1 ♯5 1 3

E°
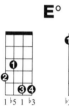

1 ♭5 1 ♭3   ♭3 1 ♭3 ♭5

E5
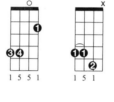

1 5 5 1   1 5 1

Eadd9
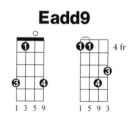

1 3 5 9   1 5 9 3

Em(add9)
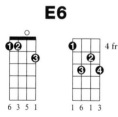

1 ♭3 5 9   1 5 9 ♭3

Esus4
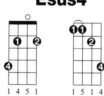

1 4 5 1   1 5 1 4

Esus2
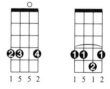

1 5 5 2   1 5 1 2

E6
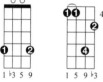

6 3 5 1   1 6 1 3

Em6
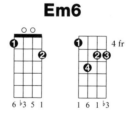

6 ♭3 5 1   1 6 1 ♭3

Emaj7
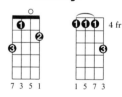

7 3 5 1   1 5 7 3

Emaj7♯5
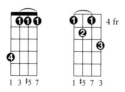

1 3 ♯5 7   1 ♯5 7 3

Emaj7♭5
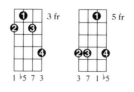

1 ♭5 7 3   3 7 1 ♭5

Emaj9
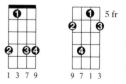

1 3 7 9   9 7 1 3

E

Emaj13
1 3 13 7   13 3 7 1

Em7
1 ♭3 5 ♭7   1 5 ♭7 ♭3

Em(maj7)
1 ♭3 5 7   1 5 7 ♭3

Em7♭5
1 ♭5 ♭7 ♭3   ♭3 ♭7 1 ♭5   5 fr

Em9
1 ♭3 ♭7 9   ♭3 ♭7 1 9   4 fr

Em11
♭7 11 1 ♭3   1 11 ♭7 ♭3

E7
1 3 5 ♭7   3 ♭7 1 5   5 fr

E7sus4
1 4 5 ♭7   4 ♭7 1 5   5 fr

E+7
♭7 3 ♯5 1   1 ♯5 ♭7 3

E7♭5
1 ♭5 ♭7 3   3 fr   3 ♭7 1 ♭5   5 fr

E9
1 3 ♭7 9   3 1 9 ♭7   7 fr

E7♯9
♯9 ♭7 1 3   5 fr   3 1 ♯9 ♭7   8 fr

E11
3 1 11 ♭7   8 fr   11 1 3 ♭7   9 fr

E13
♭7 3 13 1   3 13 1 ♭7   5 fr

E°7
1 ♭5 ♭♭7 ♭3   ♭3 ♭♭7 1 ♭5   5 fr

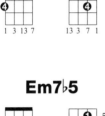

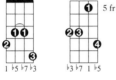
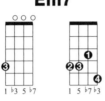
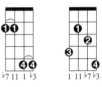
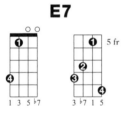

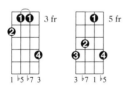
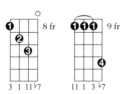
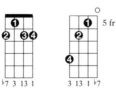

F

F

5 3 5 1 | 1 5 1 3

Fm

5 ♭3 5 1 | 1 5 1 ♭3

F+

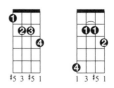

♯5 3 ♯5 1 | 1 3 ♯5 1

F°

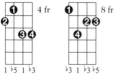

1 ♭5 1 ♭3 | ♭3 1 ♭3 ♭5

F5

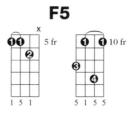

1 5 1 | 5 1 5 5

Fadd9

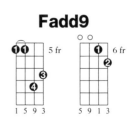

1 5 9 3 | 5 9 1 3

Fm(add9)

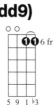

1 5 9 ♭3 | 5 9 1 ♭3

Fsus4

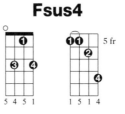

5 4 5 1 | 1 5 1 4

Fsus2

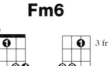

5 2 5 1 | 1 5 1 2

F6

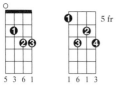

5 3 6 1 | 1 6 1 3

Fm6

5 ♭3 6 1 | 1 5 6 ♭3

Fmaj7

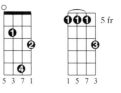

5 3 7 1 | 1 5 7 3

Fmaj7♯5

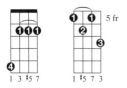

1 3 ♯5 7 | 1 ♯5 7 3

Fmaj7♭5

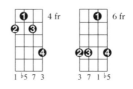

1 ♭5 7 3 | 3 7 1 ♭5

Fmaj9

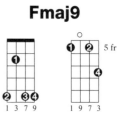

1 3 7 9 | 1 9 7 3

F

Fmaj13

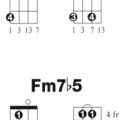

1 3 13 7   1 3 7 13

Fm7

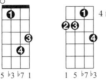

5 ♭3 ♭7 1   1 5 ♭7 ♭3

4 fr

Fm(maj7)

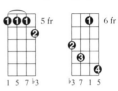

1 5 7 ♭3   ♭3 7 1 5

5 fr   6 fr

Fm7♭5

♭7 ♭3 ♭5 1   1 ♭5 ♭3

4 fr

Fm9

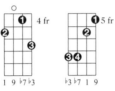

1 9 ♭7 ♭3   ♭3 ♭7 1 9

4 fr   5 fr

Fm11

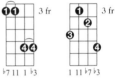

♭7 11 1 ♭3   1 11 ♭7 ♭3

3 fr   3 fr

F7

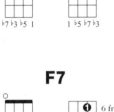

5 3 ♭7 1   3 ♭7 1 5

6 fr

F7sus4

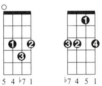

5 4 ♭7 1   ♭7 4 5 1

F+7

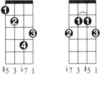

♯5 3 ♭7 1   ♭7 3 ♯5 1

F7♭5

♭7 3 ♭5 1   1 ♭5 ♭7 3

4 fr

F9

1 3 ♭7 9   1 9 ♭7 3

4 fr

F7♯9

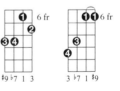

♯9 ♭7 1 3   3 ♭7 1 ♯9

6 fr   6 fr

F11

♭7 11 1 3   11 1 3 ♭7

3 fr   10 fr

F13

♭7 3 13 1   1 3 ♭7 13

F°7

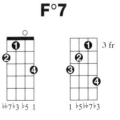

♭♭7 ♭3 ♭5 1   1 ♭5 ♭♭7 ♭3

3 fr

F#

F#

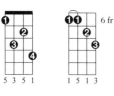

5 3 5 1   1 5 1 3   6 fr

F#m

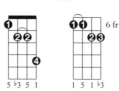

5 ♭3 5 1   1 5 1 ♭3   6 fr

F#+

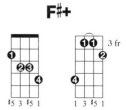

#5 3 #5 1   1 3 #5 1   3 fr

F#°

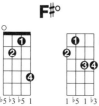

♭5 ♭3 ♭5 1   1 ♭5 1 ♭3   5 fr

F#5

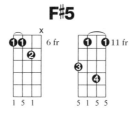

1 5 1   5 1 5 5   6 fr / 11 fr

F#add9

1 5 9 3   9 5 1 3   6 fr / 6 fr

F#m(add9)

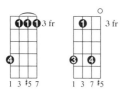

1 5 9 ♭3   9 5 1 ♭3   6 fr

F#sus4

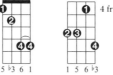

1 5 4 1   1 5 1 4   4 fr / 6 fr

F#sus2

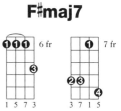

5 2 5 1   1 5 1 2   6 fr

F#6

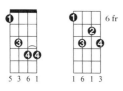

5 3 6 1   1 6 1 3   6 fr

F#m6

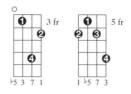

5 ♭3 6 1   1 5 6 ♭3   4 fr

F#maj7

1 5 7 3   3 7 1 5   6 fr / 7 fr

F#maj7#5

1 3 #5 7   1 3 7 #5   3 fr / 3 fr

F#maj7♭5

♭5 3 7 1   1 ♭5 7 3   3 fr / 5 fr

F#maj9

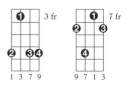

1 3 7 9   9 7 1 3   3 fr / 7 fr

F#maj13

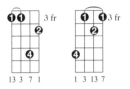

13 3 7 1   1 3 13 7

F#m7

b7 b3 5 1   1 5 b7 b3

F#m(maj7)

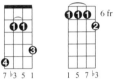
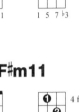

7 b3 5 1   1 5 7 b3

F#m7b5

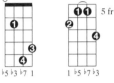

b5 b3 b7 1   1 b5 b7 b3

F#m9

b3 b7 1 9   9 b7 1 b3

F#m11

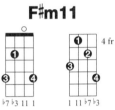

b7 b3 11 1   1 11 b7 b3

F#7

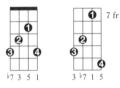

b7 3 5 1   3 b7 1 5

F#7sus4

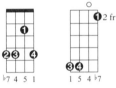

b7 4 5 1   1 5 4 b7

F#+7

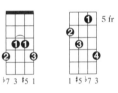

b7 3 #5 1   1 #5 b7 3

F#7b5

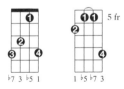

b7 3 b5 1   1 b5 b7 3

F#9

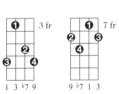

1 3 b7 9   9 b7 1 3

F#7#9

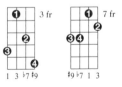

1 3 b7 #9   #9 b7 1 3

F#11

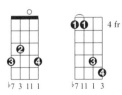

b7 3 11 1   b7 11 1 3

F#13

b7 3 13 1   1 13 b7 3

F#°7

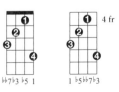

bb7 b3 b5 1   1 b5 bb7 b3

45

G

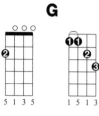

5 1 3 5   1 5 1 3

Gm

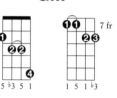

5 ♭3 5 1   1 5 1 ♭3

G+

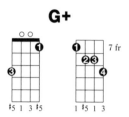

♯5 1 3 ♯5   1 ♯5 1 3

G°

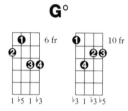

1 ♭5 1 ♭3   ♭3 1 ♭3 ♭5

G5

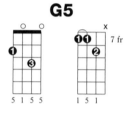

5 1 5 5   1 5 1

Gadd9

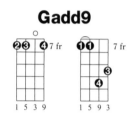

1 5 3 9   1 5 9 3

Gm(add9)

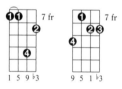

1 5 9 ♭3   9 5 1 ♭3

Gsus4

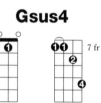

5 1 4 5   1 5 1 4

Gsus2

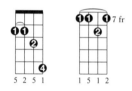

5 2 5 1   1 5 1 2

G6

5 1 3 6   5 3 6 1

Gm6

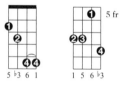

5 ♭3 6 1   1 5 6 ♭3

Gmaj7

5 1 3 7   1 5 7 3

Gmaj7♯5

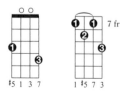

♯5 1 3 7   1 ♯5 7 3

Gmaj7♭5

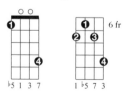

♭5 1 3 7   1 ♭5 7 3

Gmaj9

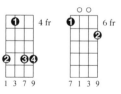

1 3 7 9   7 1 3 9

G

Gmaj13

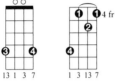

13 1 3 7   1 3 13 7

Gm7

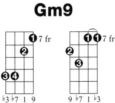

6 fr

♭7 ♭3 5 1   1 5 ♭7 ♭3

Gm(maj7)

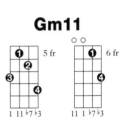

3 fr   7 fr

7 ♭3 5 1   1 5 7 ♭3

Gm7♭5

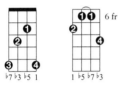

6 fr

♭7 ♭3 ♭5 1   1 ♭5 ♭7 ♭3

Gm9

7 fr   7 fr

♭3 ♭7 1 9   9 ♭7 1 ♭3

Gm11

5 fr   6 fr

1 11 ♭7 ♭3   11 1 ♭7 ♭3

G7

5 1 3 ♭7   ♭7 3 5 1

G7sus4

5 1 4 ♭7   ♭7 4 5 1

G+7

♯5 1 3 ♭7   ♭7 3 ♯5 1

G7♭5

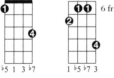

6 fr

♭5 1 3 ♭7   1 ♭5 ♭7 3

G9

7 fr

♭7 9 3 1   1 5 9 3

G7♯9

8 fr

♭7 ♯9 3 1   ♯9 ♭7 1 3

G11

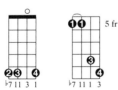

5 fr

♭7 11 3 1   ♭7 11 1 3

G13

♭7 1 3 13   ♭7 3 13 1

G°7

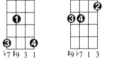
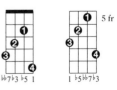

5 fr

♭♭7 ♭3 ♭5 1   1 ♭5 ♭♭7 ♭3

47

A♭

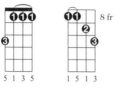

A♭m

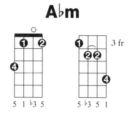

A♭+

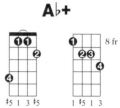

A♭°

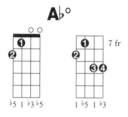

A♭5

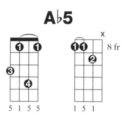

A♭add9

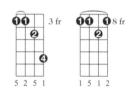

A♭m(add9)

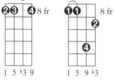

A♭sus4

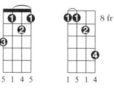

A♭sus2

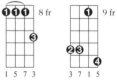

A♭6

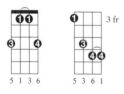

A♭m6

A♭maj7

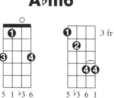

A♭maj7♯5

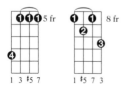

A♭maj7♭5

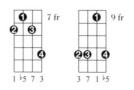

A♭maj9

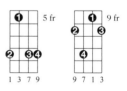

A♭maj13

13 3 7 1   1 3 13 7

A♭m7

5 1 ♭3 ♭7   1 5 ♭7 ♭3

A♭m(maj7)

7 ♭3 5 1   1 5 7 ♭3

A♭m7♭5

♭5 1 ♭3 ♭7   1 ♭5 ♭7 ♭3

A♭m9

♭7 9 ♭3 1   ♭3 ♭7 1 9

A♭m11

♭7 11 ♭3 1   1 11 ♭7 ♭3

A♭7

5 1 3 ♭7   ♭7 3 5 1

A♭7sus4

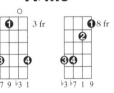

5 1 4 ♭7   ♭7 4 5 1

A♭+7

♯5 1 3 ♭7   ♭7 3 ♯5 1

A♭7♭5

♭5 1 3 ♭7   1 3 ♭7 ♭5

A♭9

1 3 ♭7 9   1 ♭7 9 3

A♭7♯9

1 3 ♭7 ♯9   ♭7 3 ♯9 1

A♭11

11 1 3 ♭7   ♭7 11 1 3

A♭13

♭7 3 13 1   1 13 ♭7 3

A♭°7

♭5 1 ♭3 ♭♭7   1 ♭5♭♭7 ♭3

49

A

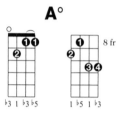

```
3 1 3 5      1 5 1 3   9 fr
```

Am

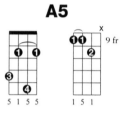

```
♭3 1 ♭3 5    1 5 1 ♭3   9 fr
```

A+

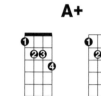

```
3 1 3 ♯5     1 ♯5 1 3   9 fr
```

A°

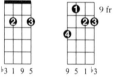

```
♭3 1 ♭3 ♭5   1 ♭5 1 ♭3   8 fr
```

A5

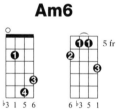

```
5 1 5 5      1 5 1    9 fr
```

Aadd9

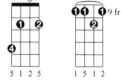

```
3 1 9 5      9 5 1 3   9 fr
```

Am(add9)

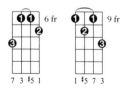

```
♭3 1 9 5     9 5 1 ♭3   9 fr
```

Asus4

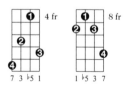

```
5 1 4 4      1 5 1 4   9 fr
```

Asus2

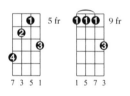

```
5 1 2 5      1 5 1 2   9 fr
```

A6

```
3 1 3 6      5 1 3 6
```

Am6

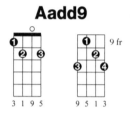

```
♭3 1 5 6     6 ♭3 5 1   5 fr
```

Amaj7

```
7 3 5 1      1 5 7 3   5 fr   9 fr
```

Amaj7♯5

```
7 3 ♯5 1     1 ♯5 7 3   6 fr   9 fr
```

Amaj7♭5

```
7 3 ♭5 1     1 ♭5 3 7   4 fr   8 fr
```

Amaj9

```
7 3 9 1      1 3 7 9    6 fr   6 fr
```

A

Amaj13
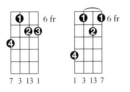

Am7
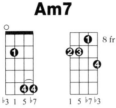

Am(maj7)
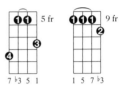

Am7♭5

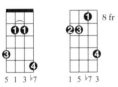

Am9
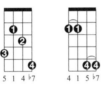

Am11
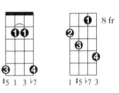

A7

A7sus4

A+7
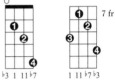

A7♭5

A9

A7#9

A11
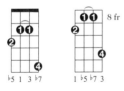

A13
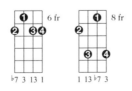

A°7
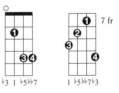

B♭

3 1 3 5   1 5 1 3   10 fr

B♭m

♭3 1 ♭3 5   1 5 1 ♭3   10 fr

B♭+

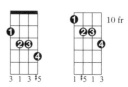

3 1 3 #5   1 #5 1 3   10 fr

B♭°

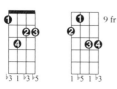

♭3 1 ♭3 ♭5   1 ♭5 1 ♭3   9 fr

B♭5

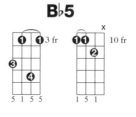

5 1 5 5   1 5 1   3 fr / 10 fr

B♭add9

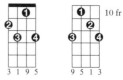

3 1 9 5   9 5 1 3   10 fr

B♭m(add9)

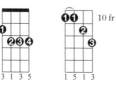

♭3 1 9 5   9 1 ♭3 5

B♭sus4

4 1 4 5   1 5 1 4   10 fr

B♭sus2

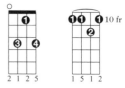

2 1 2 5   1 5 1 2   10 fr

B♭6

3 1 3 6   5 1 3 6

B♭m6

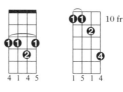

5 ♭3 6 1   6 ♭3 5 1   5 fr / 6 fr

B♭maj7

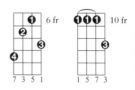

7 3 5 1   1 5 7 3   6 fr / 10 fr

B♭maj7♯5

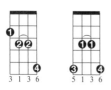

7 3 #5 1   1 #5 7 3   7 fr / 10 fr

B♭maj7♭5

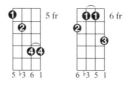

7 3 ♭5 1   1 ♭5 7 3   5 fr / 9 fr

B♭maj9

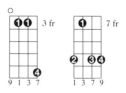

9 1 3 7   1 3 7 9   3 fr / 7 fr

B♭

B♭maj13
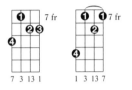
7 3 13 1   1 3 13 7

B♭m7
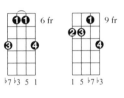
♭7 ♭3 5 1   1 5 ♭7 ♭3

B♭m(maj7)
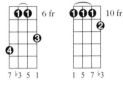
7 ♭3 5 1   1 5 7 ♭3

B♭m7♭5
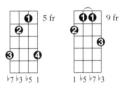
♭7 ♭3 ♭5 1   1 ♭5 ♭7 ♭3

B♭m9
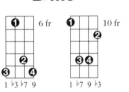
1 ♭3 ♭7 9   1 ♭7 9 ♭3

B♭m11
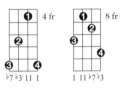
♭7 ♭3 11 1   1 11 ♭7 ♭3

B♭7
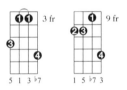
5 1 3 ♭7   1 5 ♭7 3

B♭7sus4
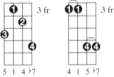
5 1 4 ♭7   4 1 5 ♭7

B♭+7
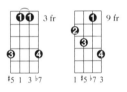
♯5 1 3 ♭7   1 ♯5 ♭7 3

B♭7♭5
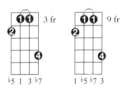
♭5 1 3 ♭7   1 ♭5 ♭7 3

B♭9
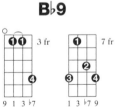
9 1 3 ♭7   1 3 ♭7 9

B♭7♯9
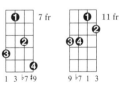
1 3 ♭7 ♯9   9 ♭7 1 3

B♭11
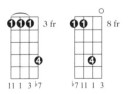
11 1 3 ♭7   ♭7 11 1 3

B♭13
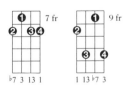
♭7 3 13 1   1 13 ♭7 3

B♭°7
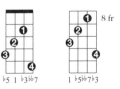
♭5 1 ♭3 ♭♭7   1 ♭5 ♭♭7 ♭3

53

B

B

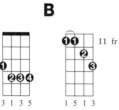

3 1 3 5   1 5 1 3

Bm

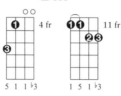

5 1 1 ♭3   1 5 1 ♭3

B+

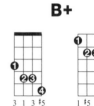

3 1 3 ♯5   1 ♯5 1 3

B°

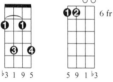

♭5 1 1 ♭3   1 ♭5 1 ♭3

B5

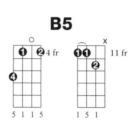

5 1 1 5   1 5 1

Badd9

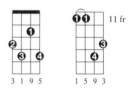

3 1 9 5   1 5 9 3

Bm(add9)

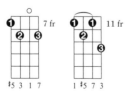

♭3 1 9 5   5 9 1 ♭3

Bsus4

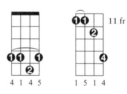

4 1 4 5   1 5 1 4

Bsus2

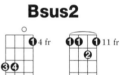

5 2 1 5   1 5 1 2

B6

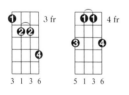

3 1 3 6   5 1 3 6

Bm6

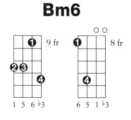

1 5 6 ♭3   6 5 1 ♭3

Bmaj7

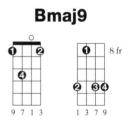

5 3 1 7   1 5 7 3

Bmaj7♯5

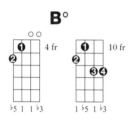

♯5 3 1 7   1 ♯5 7 3

Bmaj7♭5

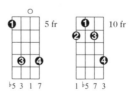

♭5 3 1 7   1 ♭5 7 3

Bmaj9

9 7 1 3   1 3 7 9

B

Bmaj13

Bm7
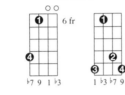

Bm(maj7)
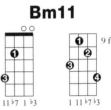

Bm7♭5
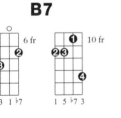

Bm9
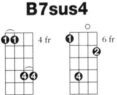

Bm11
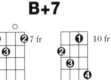

B7
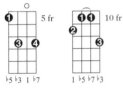

B7sus4

B+7
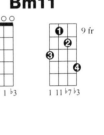

B7♭5
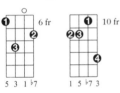

B9
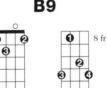

B7#9

B11
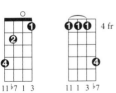

B13
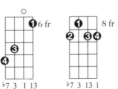

B°7
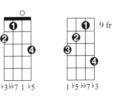

C

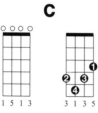
1 5 1 3   3 1 3 5

Cm
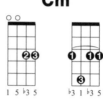
1 5 ♭3 5   ♭3 1 ♭3 5

C+
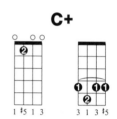
1 ♯5 1 3   3 1 3 ♯5

C°
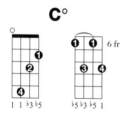
1 1 ♭3 ♭5   ♭5 ♭3 ♭5 1

C5
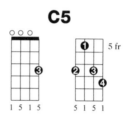
1 5 1 5   5 1 5 1

Cadd9
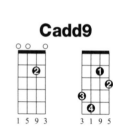
1 5 9 3   3 1 9 5

Cm(add9)
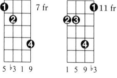
5 ♭3 1 9   1 5 9 ♭3

Csus4
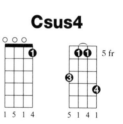
1 5 1 4   5 1 4 1

Csus2
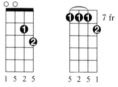
1 5 2 5   5 2 5 1

C6

1 6 3 5   1 5 6 3

Cm6
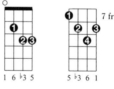
1 6 ♭3 5   5 ♭3 6 1

Cmaj7

1 7 3 5   1 5 7 3

Cmaj7♯5
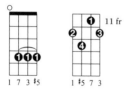
1 7 3 ♯5   1 ♯5 7 3

Cmaj7♭5

1 7 3 ♭5   1 ♭5 7 3

Cmaj9
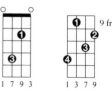
1 7 9 3   1 3 7 9

56

C

Cmaj13

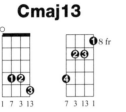

1 7 3 13   7 3 13 1

Cm7

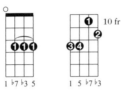

1 ♭7 ♭3 5   1 5 ♭7 ♭3

Cm(maj7)

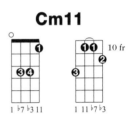

1 7 ♭3 5   1 5 7 ♭3

Cm7♭5

1 ♭7 ♭3 ♭5   1 ♭5 ♭7 ♭3

Cm9

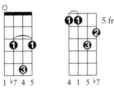

1 ♭3 ♭7 9   ♭7 ♭3 1 9

Cm11

1 ♭7 ♭3 11   1 11 ♭7 ♭3

C7

1 ♭7 3 5   3 1 5 ♭7

C7sus4

1 ♭7 4 5   4 1 5 ♭7

C+7

1 ♭7 3 ♯5   ♭7 3 ♯5 1

C7♭5

1 ♭7 3 ♭5   3 1 ♭5 ♭7

C9

1 ♭7 9 3   ♭7 3 1 9

C7♯9

1 ♭7 ♯9 3   ♭7 3 1 ♯9

C11

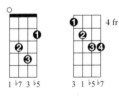

1 ♭7 11 3   1 11 ♭7 3

C13

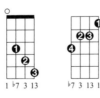

1 ♭7 3 13   ♭7 3 13 1

C°7

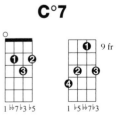

1 ♭♭7 ♭3 ♭5   1 ♭5 ♭♭7 ♭3

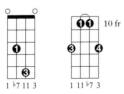
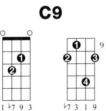
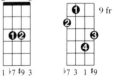

57

D♭

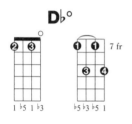

1 5 1 3   3 1 3 5

D♭m

1 5 1♭3   ♭3 1 ♭3 5

D♭+

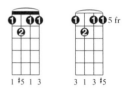

1 ♯5 1 3   3 1 3 ♯5

D♭°

1 ♭5 1 ♭3   ♭5 ♭3 ♭5 1

D♭5

1 5 1 5   5 1 5 1

D♭add9

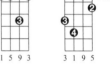

1 5 9 3   3 1 9 5

D♭m(add9)

1 5 9 ♭3   ♭3 1 9 5

D♭sus4

1 5 1 4   5 1 4 1

D♭sus2

1 5 2 5   5 2 5 1

D♭6

3 1 5 6   1 5 6 3

D♭m6

1 6 ♭3 5   5 1 6 ♭3

D♭maj7

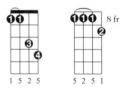

1 5 7 3   3 1 5 7

D♭maj7♯5

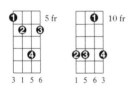

1 ♯5 7 3   ♯5 3 7 1

D♭maj7♭5

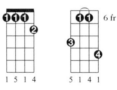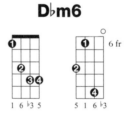

1 ♭5 7 3   3 1 ♭5 7

D♭maj9

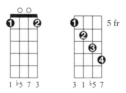

7 3 1 9   1 3 7 9

D♭

D♭maj13

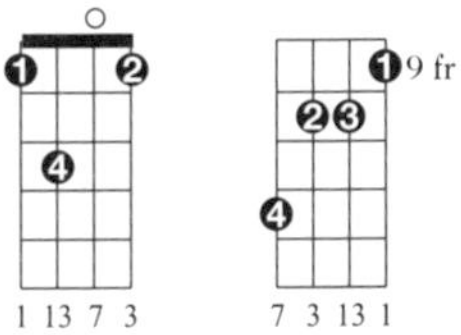
9 fr
1 13 7 3
7 3 13 1

D♭m7

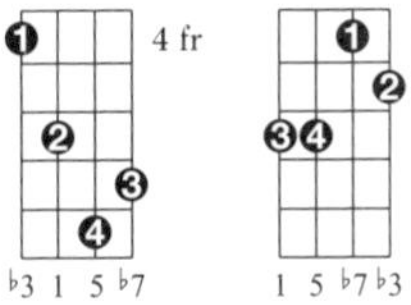
4 fr
11 fr
♭3 1 5 ♭7
1 5 ♭7 ♭3

D♭m(maj7)

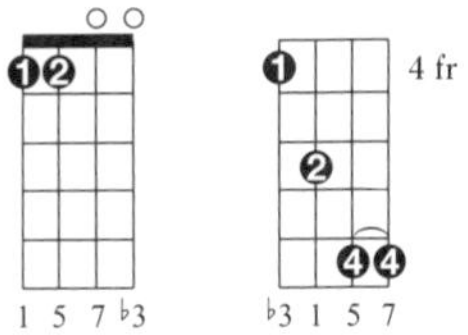
4 fr
1 5 7 ♭3
♭3 1 5 7

D♭m7♭5

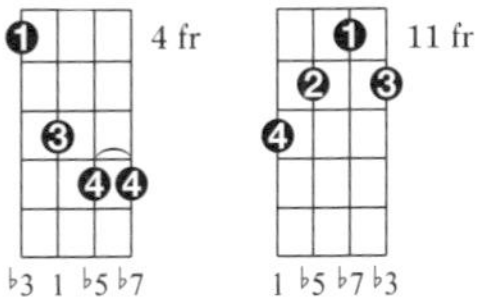
4 fr
11 fr
♭3 1 ♭5 ♭7
1 ♭5 ♭7 ♭3

D♭m9

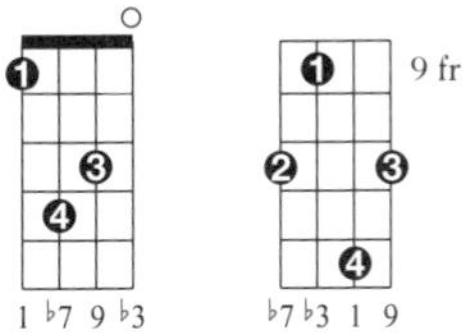
9 fr
1 ♭7 9 ♭3
♭7 ♭3 1 9

D♭m11

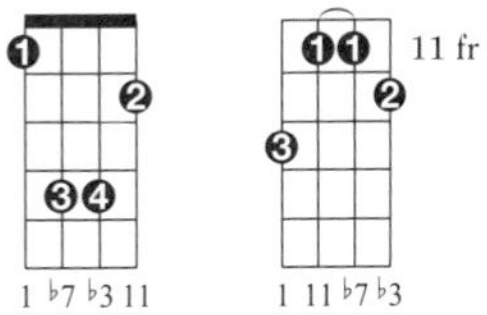
11 fr
1 ♭7 ♭3 11
1 11 ♭7 ♭3

D♭7

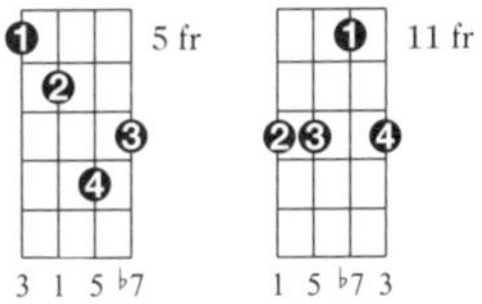
5 fr
11 fr
3 1 5 ♭7
1 5 ♭7 3

D♭7sus4

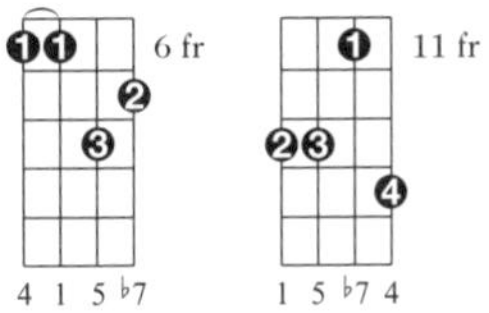
6 fr
11 fr
4 1 5 ♭7
1 5 ♭7 4

D♭+7

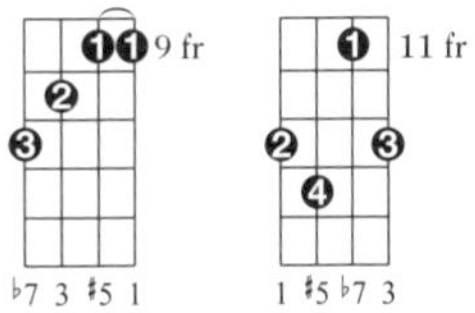
9 fr
11 fr
♭7 3 ♯5 1
1 ♯5 ♭7 3

D♭7♭5

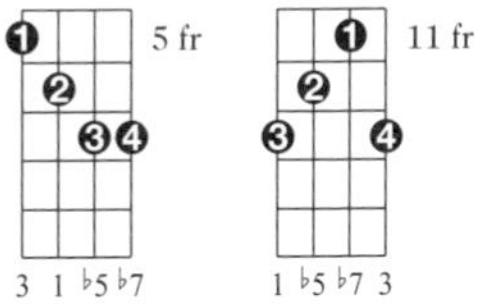
5 fr
11 fr
3 1 ♭5 ♭7
1 ♭5 ♭7 3

D♭9

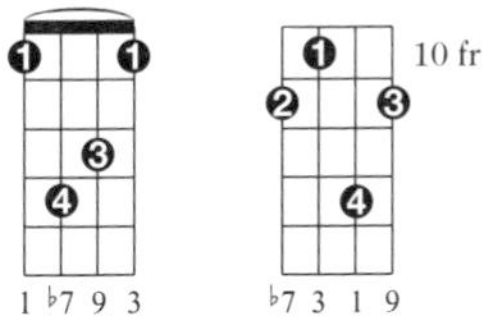
10 fr
1 ♭7 9 3
♭7 3 1 9

D♭7♯9

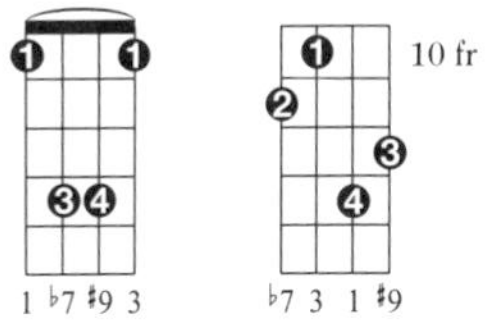
10 fr
1 ♭7 ♯9 3
♭7 3 1 ♯9

D♭11

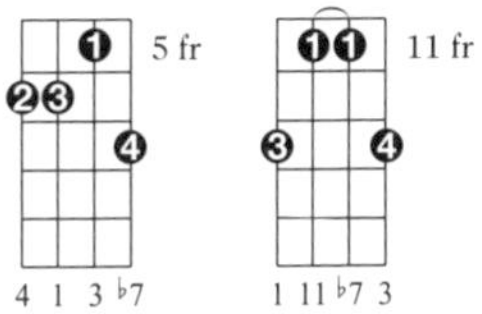
5 fr
11 fr
4 1 3 ♭7
1 11 ♭7 3

D♭13

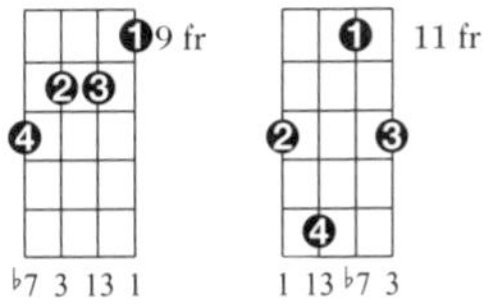
9 fr
11 fr
♭7 3 13 1
1 13 ♭7 3

D♭°7

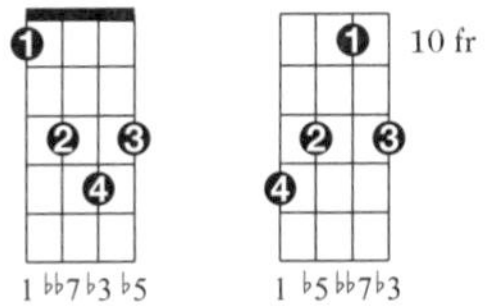
10 fr
1 ♭♭7 ♭3 ♭5
1 ♭5 ♭♭7 ♭3

D

D

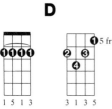

1 5 1 3   3 1 3 5

Dm

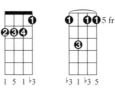

1 5 1 ♭3   ♭3 1 ♭3 5

D+

1 ♯5 1 3   3 1 3 ♯5

D°

1 ♭5 1 ♭3   ♭5 ♭3 ♭5 1

D5

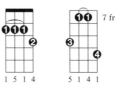

1 5 1 5   5 1 5 1

Dadd9

1 5 9 3   3 1 5 9

Dm(add9)

♭3 1 9 5   ♭3 1 5 9

Dsus4

1 5 1 4   5 1 4 1

Dsus2

1 5 1 2   1 5 2 5

D6

3 1 5 6   1 5 6 3

Dm6

1 6 ♭3 5   5 1 ♭3 6

Dmaj7

1 5 7 3   3 1 5 7

Dmaj7♯5

1 ♯5 7 3   ♯5 3 7 1

Dmaj7♭5

1 ♭5 7 3   3 1 ♭5 7

Dmaj9

7 3 1 9   1 3 7 9

60

D

Dmaj13
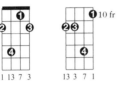
1 13 7 3   13 3 7 1

Dm7
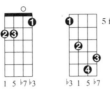
1 5 ♭7 ♭3   ♭3 1 5 ♭7

Dm(maj7)
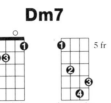
1 5 7 ♭3   ♭3 1 5 7

Dm7♭5
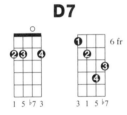
1 ♭5 ♭7 ♭3   ♭3 1 ♭5 ♭7

Dm9
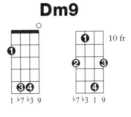
1 ♭7 ♭3 9   ♭7 ♭3 1 9

Dm11
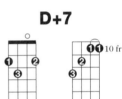
1 11 ♭7 ♭3   1 ♭7 ♭3 11

D7
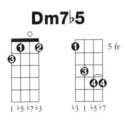
1 5 ♭7 3   3 1 5 ♭7

D7sus4
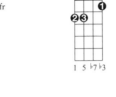
1 5 ♭7 4   4 1 5 ♭7

D+7

1 ♯5 ♭7 3   ♭7 3 ♯5 1

D7♭5

1 ♭5 ♭7 3   3 1 ♭5 ♭7

D9
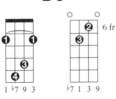
1 ♭7 9 3   ♭7 1 3 9

D7♯9
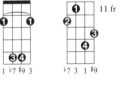
1 ♭7 ♯9 3   ♭7 3 1 ♯9

D11
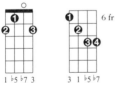
1 11 ♭7 3   11 1 3 ♭7

D13
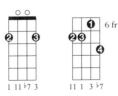
1 13 ♭7 3   ♭7 3 13 1

D°7
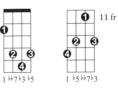
1 ♭♭7 ♭3 ♭5   1 ♭5 ♭♭7 ♭3

E♭

E♭

1 5 1 3   3 1 3 5

E♭m

1 5 1♭3   ♭3 1 ♭3 5

E♭+

1 ♯5 1 3   3 1 3 ♯5

E♭°

1 ♭5 1 ♭3   ♭5 ♭3 ♭5 1

E♭5

1 5 1 5   5 1 5 1

E♭add9

1 5 9 3   9 5 1 3

E♭m(add9)

♭3 1 9 5   9 1 ♭3 5

E♭sus4

1 5 1 4   5 1 4 1

E♭sus2

1 5 1 2   1 5 2 5

E♭6

1 5 6 3   3 1 5 6

E♭m6

1 5 6 ♭3   1 6 ♭3 5

E♭maj7

1 5 7 3   3 1 5 7

E♭maj7♯5

1 ♯5 7 3   ♯5 3 7 1

E♭maj7♭5

1 ♭5 7 3   3 1 ♭5 7

E♭maj9

1 3 7 9   7 3 1 9

E♭maj13

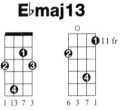

1 13 7 3   6 3 7 1

E♭m7

1 5 ♭7 ♭3   ♭3 1 5 ♭7

E♭m(maj7)

1 5 7 ♭3   ♭3 1 5 7

E♭m7♭5

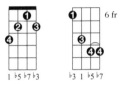

1 ♭5 ♭7 ♭3   ♭3 1 ♭5 ♭7

E♭m9

9 1 ♭3 ♭7   ♭7 ♭3 1 9

E♭m11

1 11 ♭7 ♭3   1 ♭7 ♭3 11

E♭7

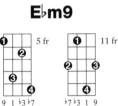

1 5 ♭7 ♭3   3 1 5 ♭7

E♭7sus4

1 5 ♭7 4   4 1 5 ♭7

E♭+7

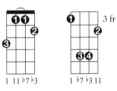

1 ♯5 ♭7 3   ♭7 3 ♯5 1

E♭7♭5

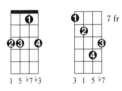

1 ♭5 ♭7 3   3 1 ♭5 ♭7

E♭9

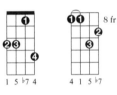

1 3 ♭7 9   1 ♭7 9 3

E♭7♯9

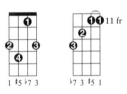

1 3 ♭7 ♯9   1 ♭7 ♯9 3

E♭11

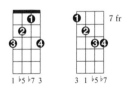

1 11 ♭7 3   1 3 ♭7 11

E♭13

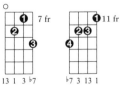

13 1 3 ♭7   ♭7 3 13 1

E♭°7

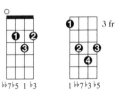

♭♭7 ♭5 1 ♭3   1 ♭♭7 ♭3 ♭5

E

E

Em
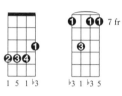

E+
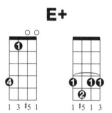

E°
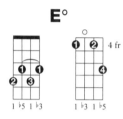

E5
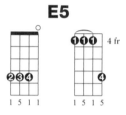

Eadd9
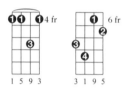

Em(add9)
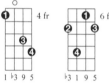

Esus4
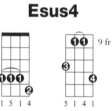

Esus2
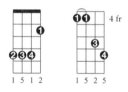

E6
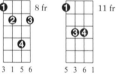

Em6

Emaj7
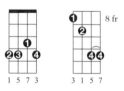

Emaj7#5
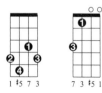

Emaj7♭5

Emaj9

E

Emaj13
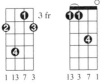

1 13 7 3   13 3 7 1

Em7
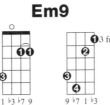

1 5 ♭7 ♭3   ♭3 1 5 ♭7

Em(maj7)
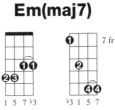

1 5 7 ♭3   ♭3 1 5 7

Em7♭5

1 ♭5 ♭7 ♭3   ♭3 1 ♭5 ♭7

Em9
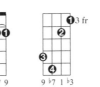

1 ♭3 ♭7 9   9 ♭7 1 ♭3

Em11

1 11 ♭7 ♭3   1 ♭3 ♭7 11

E7
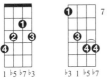

1 5 ♭7 3   3 1 5 ♭7

E7sus4
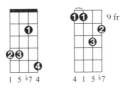

1 5 ♭7 4   4 1 5 ♭7

E+7
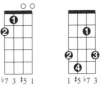

♭7 3 ♯5 1   1 ♯5 ♭7 3

E7♭5
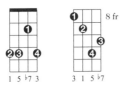

1 ♭5 7 3   3 1 ♭5 ♭7

E9
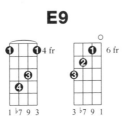

1 ♭7 9 3   3 ♭7 9 1

E7♯9
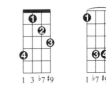

1 3 ♭7 ♯9   1 ♭7 ♯9 3

E11
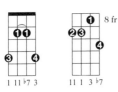

1 11 ♭7 3   11 1 3 ♭7

E13

♭7 3 13 1   13 3 ♭7 1

E°7
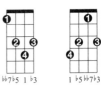

♭♭7 ♭5 1 ♭3   1 ♭5 ♭♭7 ♭3

F

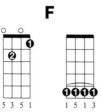

5 3 5 1   1 5 1 3

Fm

5 ♭3 5 1   1 5 1 ♭3

F+

5 fr

♯5 3 ♯5 1   1 ♯5 1 3

F°

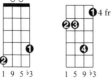

1 ♭5 1 ♭3   ♭5 ♭3 ♭5 1   11 fr

F5

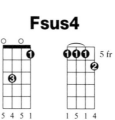

5 fr   10 fr

1 5 1 5   5 1 5 1

Fadd9

5 fr

1 3 5 9   1 5 9 3

Fm(add9)

4 fr

1 9 5 ♭3   1 5 9 ♭3

Fsus4

5 fr

5 4 5 1   1 5 1 4

Fsus2

1 2 5 1   1 5 1 2

F6

9 fr

5 3 6 1   3 1 5 6

Fm6

5 fr

5 ♭3 6 1   1 6 ♭3 5

Fmaj7

5 3 7 1   1 5 7 3

Fmaj7♯5

4 fr

♯5 3 7 1   1 ♯5 7 3

Fmaj7♭5

9 fr

1 ♭5 7 3   3 1 ♭5 7

Fmaj9

1 9 7 3   1 3 7 9

F

Fmaj13
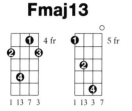

1 13 7 3   1 13 3 7

Fm7
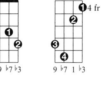

5 ♭3 ♭7 1   1 5 ♭7 3

Fm(maj7)
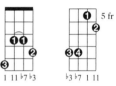

5 ♭3 7 1   1 5 7 ♭3

Fm7♭5
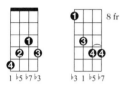

1 ♭5 ♭7 ♭3   ♭3 1 ♭5 ♭7

Fm9
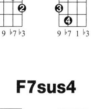

1 9 ♭7 ♭3   9 ♭7 1 ♭3

Fm11
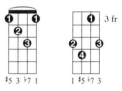

1 11 ♭7 ♭3   ♭3 ♭7 1 11

F7
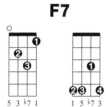

5 3 ♭7 1   1 5 ♭7 3

F7sus4
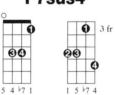

5 4 ♭7 1   1 5 ♭7 4

F+7
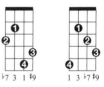

♯5 3 ♭7 1   1 ♯5 ♭7 3

F7♭5
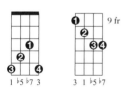

1 ♭5 ♭7 3   3 1 ♭5 ♭7

F9

1 9 ♭7 3   1 ♭7 9 3

F7♯9

♭7 3 1 ♯9   1 3 ♭7 ♯9

F11
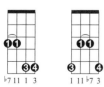

♭7 11 1 3   1 11 ♭7 3

F13

13 3 ♭7 1   ♭7 3 13 1

F°7

♭♭7 ♭5 1 ♭3   1 ♭5 ♭♭7 ♭3

F#

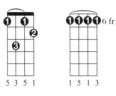

5 3 5 1   1 5 1 3

F#m

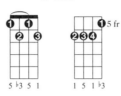

5 ♭3 5 1   1 5 1 ♭3

F#+

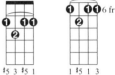

♯5 3 ♯5 1   1 ♯5 1 3

F#°

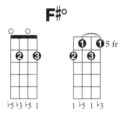

♭5 ♭3 ♯5 1   1 ♭5 1 ♭3

F#5

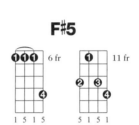

1 5 1 5   5 1 5 1

F#add9

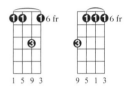

1 5 9 3   9 5 1 3

F#m(add9)

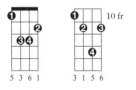

1 5 9 ♭3   ♭3 1 9 5

F#sus4

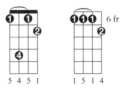

5 4 5 1   1 5 1 4

F#sus2

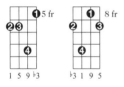

5 2 5 1   1 5 1 2

F#6

5 3 6 1   3 1 5 6

F#m6

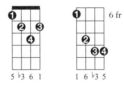

5 ♭3 6 1   1 6 ♭3 5

F#maj7

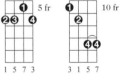

1 5 7 3   3 1 5 7

F#maj7#5

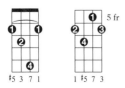

♯5 3 7 1   1 ♯5 7 3

F#maj7♭5

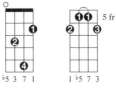

♭5 3 7 1   1 ♭5 7 3

F#maj9

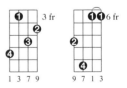

1 3 7 9   9 7 1 3

F#

F#maj13

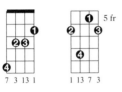

7 3 13 1   1 13 7 3

F#m7

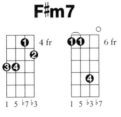

4 fr   6 fr

1 5 ♭7 3   1 5 ♭3 ♭7

F#m(maj7)

5 fr   9 fr

1 5 7 3   ♭3 1 5 7

F#m7♭5

4 fr   9 fr

1 ♭5 ♭7 3   ♭3 1 ♭5 ♭7

F#m9

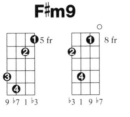

5 fr   8 fr

9 ♭7 1 ♭3   ♭3 1 9 ♭7

F#m11

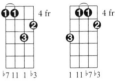

4 fr   4 fr

♭7 11 1 ♭3   1 11 ♭7 3

F#7

4 fr

5 3 ♭7 1   1 5 ♭7 3

F#7sus4

4 fr

♭7 4 5 1   1 5 ♭7 4

F#+7

4 fr

#5 3 ♭7 1   1 #5 7 3

F#7♭5

4 fr

♭5 3 ♭7 1   1 ♭5 7 3

F#9

6 fr   8 fr

1 ♭7 9 3   3 1 9 ♭7

F#7#9

3 fr   3 fr

♭7 3 1 #9   1 3 ♭7 #9

F#11

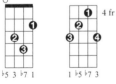

4 fr   4 fr

♭7 11 1 3   1 11 ♭7 3

F#13

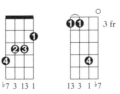

3 fr

♭7 3 13 1   13 3 1 ♭7

F#°7

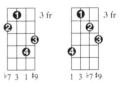
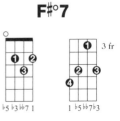

3 fr

♭5 ♭3 ♭♭7 1   1 ♭5 ♭♭7 ♭3

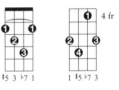
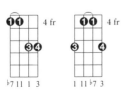
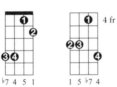

69

G

G

5 3 5 1   1 5 1 3   7 fr

Gm

5 ♭3 5 1   1 5 1 ♭3   6 fr

G+
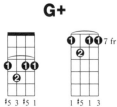

♯5 3 ♯5 1   1 ♯5 1 3   7 fr

G°
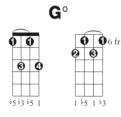

♭5 ♭3 ♭5 1   1 ♭5 1 ♭3   6 fr

G5
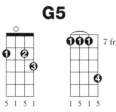

5 1 5 1   1 5 1 5   7 fr

Gadd9
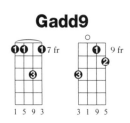

1 5 9 3   3 1 9 5   7 fr / 9 fr

Gm(add9)
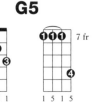

1 5 9 ♭3   ♭3 1 9 5   6 fr / 9 fr

Gsus4
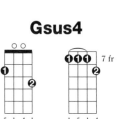

5 1 4 1   1 5 1 4   7 fr

Gsus2

5 2 5 1   1 5 1 2   5 fr

G6
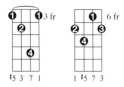

5 3 6 1   3 1 5 6   11 fr

Gm6
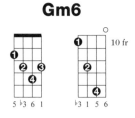

5 ♭3 6 1   ♭3 1 5 6   10 fr

Gmaj7

1 5 7 3   3 1 5 7   6 fr / 11 fr

Gmaj7♯5

♯5 3 7 1   1 ♯5 7 3   3 fr / 6 fr

Gmaj7♭5
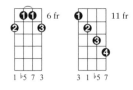

1 ♭5 7 3   3 1 ♭5 7   6 fr / 11 fr

Gmaj9
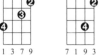

1 3 7 9   7 1 9 3   4 fr / 6 fr

G

Gmaj13
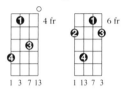
1 3 7 13   1 13 7 3

Gm7
1 5 ♭7 ♭3   ♭3 1 5 ♭7

Gm(maj7)
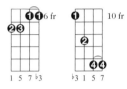
1 5 7 ♭3   ♭3 1 5 7

Gm7♭5
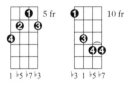
1 ♭5 ♭7 ♭3   ♭3 1 ♭5 ♭7

Gm9

9 ♭7 1 ♭3   ♭3 1 9 ♭7

Gm11
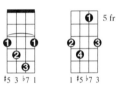
♭7 1 11 ♭3   1 11 ♭7 ♭3

G7
5 3 ♭7 1   1 5 ♭7 3

G7sus4
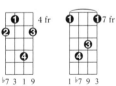
5 1 4 ♭7   1 5 ♭7 4

G+7
♯5 3 ♭7 1   1 ♯5 7 3

G7♭5
♭7 ♭5 1 3   1 ♭5 ♭7 3

G9
♭7 3 1 9   1 ♭7 9 3

G7♯9
♭7 3 1 ♯9   1 3 ♭7 ♯9

G11
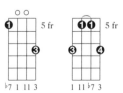
♭7 1 11 3   1 11 ♭7 3

G13
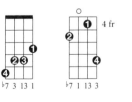
♭7 3 13 1   ♭7 1 13 3

G°7
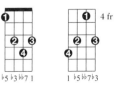
♭5 ♭3 ♭♭7 1   1 ♭5 ♭♭7 ♭3

A♭
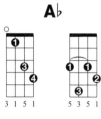

3 1 5 1   5 3 5 1

A♭m
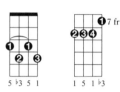

5 ♭3 5 1   1 5 1 ♭3

A♭+
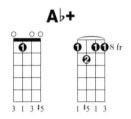

3 1 3 ♯5   1 ♯5 1 3

A♭°
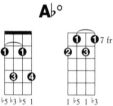

♭5 ♭3 ♭5 1   1 ♭5 1 ♭3

A♭5
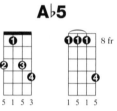

5 1 5 3   1 5 1 5

A♭add9
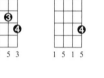

5 9 3 1   1 5 9 3

A♭m(add9)
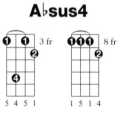

1 5 9 ♭3   9 1 ♭3 5

A♭sus4

5 4 5 1   1 5 1 4

A♭sus2
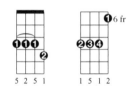

5 2 5 1   1 5 1 2

A♭6
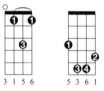

3 1 5 6   5 3 6 1

A♭m6

5 ♭3 6 1   1 6 ♭3 5

A♭maj7

3 1 5 7   1 5 7 3

A♭maj7♯5
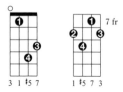

3 1 ♯5 7   1 ♯5 7 3

A♭maj7♭5
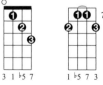

3 1 ♭5 7   1 ♭5 7 3

A♭maj9
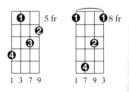

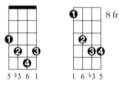

1 3 7 9   1 7 9 3

72

A♭

A♭maj13
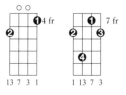

A♭m7
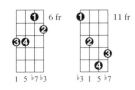

A♭m(maj7)
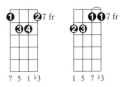

A♭m7♭5
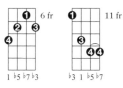

A♭m9
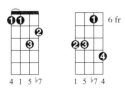

A♭m11
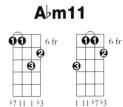

A♭7
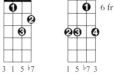

A♭7sus4
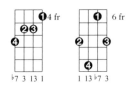

A♭+7

A♭7♭5
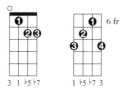

A♭9
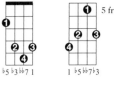

A♭7♯9

A♭11
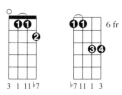

A♭13

A♭°7

A

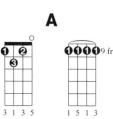
3 1 3 5   1 5 1 3

Am

3 1 3 5   1 5 1 3

A+

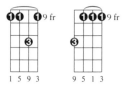
1 3 1 #5   1 #5 1 3

A°

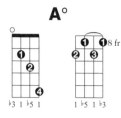
b3 1 b5 1   1 b5 1 b3

A5

b3 1 b3 5   1 5 1 b3

Aadd9

5 1 5   1 5 1 5

1 5 9 3   9 5 1 3

Am(add9)

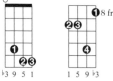
b3 9 5 1   1 5 9 b3

Asus4

4 1 4 5   1 5 1 4

Asus2

5 2 5 1   1 5 1 2

A6

3 1 5 6   1 5 6 3

Am6

b3 1 5 6   1 5 6 b3

Amaj7

3 1 5 7   1 5 7 3

Amaj7#5

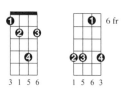
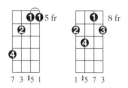
7 3 #5 1   1 #5 7 3

Amaj7b5

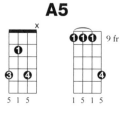
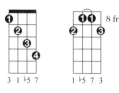
3 1 b5 7   1 b5 7 3

Amaj9

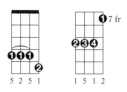
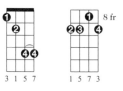
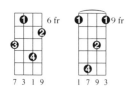
7 3 1 9   1 7 9 3

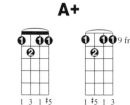

74

A

Amaj13

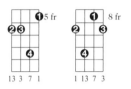

13 3 7 1   1 13 7 3

Am7

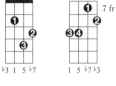

♭3 1 5 ♭7   1 5 ♭7 3

Am(maj7)

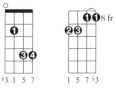

♭3 1 5 7   1 5 7 ♭3

Am7♭5

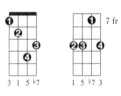

♭3 1 ♭5 ♭7   1 ♭5 ♭7 3

Am9

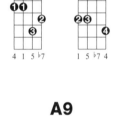

♭3 9 ♭7 1   ♭7 3 1 9

Am11

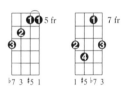

♭3 1 11 ♭7   1 11 ♭7 3

A7

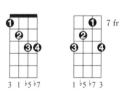

3 1 5 ♭7   1 5 ♭7 3

A7sus4

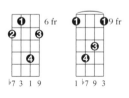

4 1 5 ♭7   1 5 ♭7 4

A+7

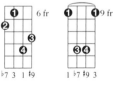

♭7 3 ♯5 1   1 ♯5 ♭7 3

A7♭5

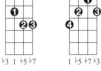

3 1 ♭5 ♭7   1 ♭5 ♭7 3

A9

♭7 3 1 9   1 ♭7 9 3

A7♯9

♭7 3 1 ♯9   1 ♭7 ♯9 3

A11

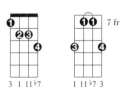

3 1 11 ♭7   1 11 ♭7 3

A13

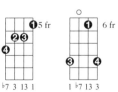

♭7 3 13 1   1 ♭7 13 3

A°7

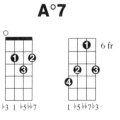

♭3 1 ♭5 ♭♭7   1 ♭5 ♭♭7 ♭3

B♭

B♭
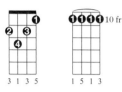

3 1 3 5   1 5 1 3

B♭m

♭3 1 ♭3 5   1 5 1 ♭3

B♭+
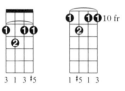

3 1 3 ♯5   1 ♯5 1 3

B♭°
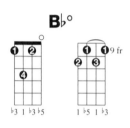

♭3 1 ♭3 ♭5   1 ♭5 1 ♭3

B♭5
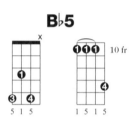

5 1 5   1 5 1 5

B♭add9
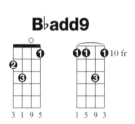

3 1 9 5   1 5 9 3

B♭m(add9)
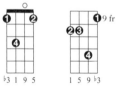

♭3 1 9 5   1 5 9 ♭3

B♭sus4
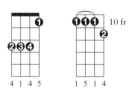

4 1 4 5   1 5 1 4

B♭sus2
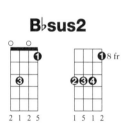

2 1 2 5   1 5 1 2

B♭6
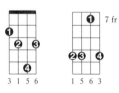

3 1 5 6   1 5 6 3

B♭m6
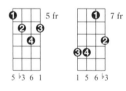

5 ♭3 6 1   1 5 6 ♭3

B♭maj7
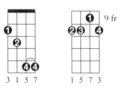

3 1 5 7   1 5 7 3

B♭maj7♯5
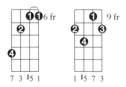

7 3 ♯5 1   1 ♯5 7 3

B♭maj7♭5

3 1 ♭5 7   1 ♭5 7 3

B♭maj9
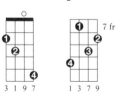

3 1 9 7   1 3 7 9

B♭

B♭maj13

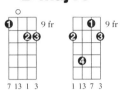

7 13 1 3   1 13 7 3

B♭m7
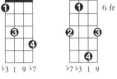

5 ♭3 ♭7 1   1 5 ♭7 ♭3

B♭m(maj7)
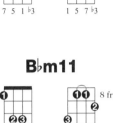

7 5 1 ♭3   1 5 7 ♭3

B♭m7♭5
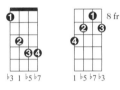

♭3 1 ♭5 ♭7   1 ♭5 ♭7 ♭3

B♭m9
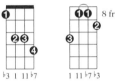

♭3 1 9 ♭7   ♭7 ♭3 1 9

B♭m11
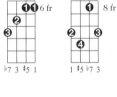

♭3 1 11 ♭7   1 11 ♭7 ♭3

B♭7
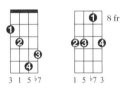

3 1 5 ♭7   1 5 ♭7 3

B♭7sus4
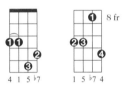

4 1 5 ♭7   1 5 ♭7 4

B♭+7
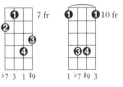

♭7 3 ♯5 1   1 ♯5 ♭7 3

B♭7♭5
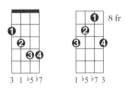

3 1 ♭5 ♭7   1 ♭5 ♭7 3

B♭9
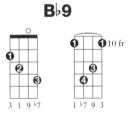

3 1 9 ♭7   1 ♭7 9 3

B♭7♯9

♭7 3 1 ♯9   1 ♭7 ♯9 3

B♭11
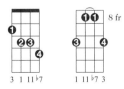

3 1 11 ♭7   1 11 ♭7 3

B♭13
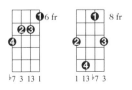

♭7 3 13 1   1 13 ♭7 3

B♭°7
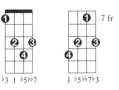

♭3 1 ♭5 ♭♭7   1 ♭5 ♭♭7 ♭3

B

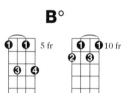

Bm

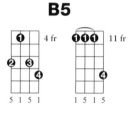

B+

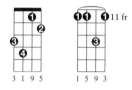

B°

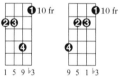

B5

Badd9

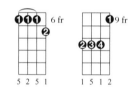

Bm(add9)

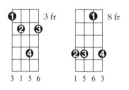

Bsus4

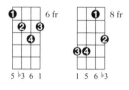

Bsus2

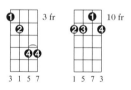

B6

Bm6

Bmaj7

Bmaj7#5

Bmaj7♭5

Bmaj9

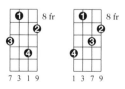

B

Bmaj13
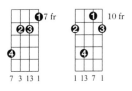
7 3 13 1　　1 13 7 1

Bm7

5 ♭3 ♭7 1　　1 5 ♭7 ♭3

Bm(maj7)
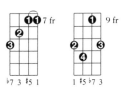
7 5 1 ♭3　　1 5 7 ♭3

Bm7♭5
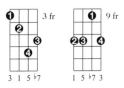
♭3 1 ♭5 ♭7　　1 ♭5 ♭7 ♭3

Bm9
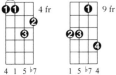
♭7 ♭3 1 9　　1 ♭7 9 ♭3

Bm11

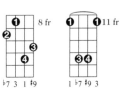
♭7 3 1 11　　1 11 ♭7 ♭3

B7
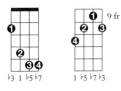
3 1 5 ♭7　　1 5 ♭7 3

B7sus4

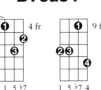
4 1 5 ♭7　　1 5 ♭7 4

B+7
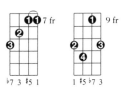
♭7 3 ♯5 1　　1 ♯5 ♭7 3

B7♭5
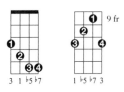
3 1 ♭5 ♭7　　1 ♭5 ♭7 3

B9
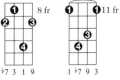
♭7 3 1 9　　1 ♭7 9 3

B7♯9
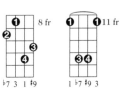
♭7 3 1 ♯9　　1 ♭7 ♯9 3

B11
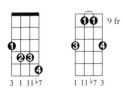
3 1 11 ♭7　　1 11 ♭7 3

B13
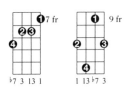
♭7 3 13 1　　1 13 ♭7 3

B°7
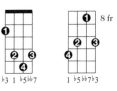
♭3 1 ♭5 ♭♭7　　1 ♭5 ♭♭7 ♭3

C

C
3 5 1 3   5 1 3 5 (5 fr)

Cm
♭3 5 1 ♭3   5 1 ♭3 5 (5 fr)

C+
3 ♯5 1 3   ♯5 1 3 ♯5 (6 fr)

C°
♭3 ♭5 1 ♭3   ♭5 1 ♭3 ♭5 (4 fr)

C5
5 1 5 (5 fr)   1 5 1 (10 fr)

Cadd9
3 5 1 9   1 3 5 9 (10 fr)

Cm(add9)
♭3 5 1 9   1 ♭3 5 9 (9 fr)

Csus4
4 5 1 4   5 1 4 5 (5 fr)

Csus2
2 5 1 2   5 1 2 5 (5 fr)

C6
3 6 1 5   5 1 3 6 (5 fr)

Cm6
5 1 ♭3 6 (5 fr)   1 ♭3 5 6 (7 fr)

Cmaj7
5 7 1 3   1 3 5 7 (9 fr)

Cmaj7♯5
♯5 1 3 7 (6 fr)   1 3 ♯5 7 (9 fr)

Cmaj7♭5
♭5 7 1 3   1 3 ♭5 7 (9 fr)

Cmaj9
3 7 1 9   1 9 3 7 (7 fr)

Cmaj13
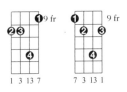

Cm7
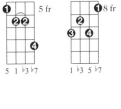

Cm(maj7)
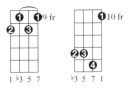

Cm7♭5
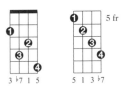

Cm9
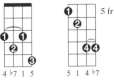

Cm11
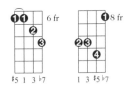

C7
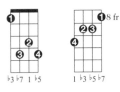

C7sus4

C+7
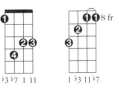

C7♭5
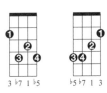

C9

C7♯9
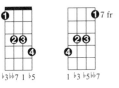

C11
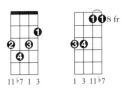

C13
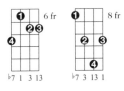

C°7
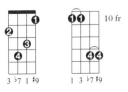

Db

3 5 1 3   5 1 3 5
6 fr

Dbm

b3 5 1 b3   5 1 b3 5
6 fr

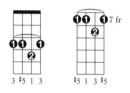

Db+

3 #5 1 3   #5 1 3 #5
7 fr

Db°

b5 1 b3 b5   1 b3 b5 1
5 fr   10 fr

Db5

5 1   5
x   x
6 fr   1 5 1
11 fr

Dbadd9

3 5 1 9   1 3 5 9
11 fr

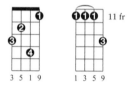

Dbm(add9)

9 5 1 b3   1 b3 5 9
10 fr

Dbsus4

4 4 1 5   5 1 4 5
4 fr   6 fr

Dbsus2

2 5 1 2   5 1 2 5
6 fr

Db6

3 6 1 5   5 1 3 6
3 fr   6 fr

Dbm6

5 1 b3 6   1 b3 5 6
6 fr   8 fr

Dbmaj7

5 7 1 3   3 7 1 5
3 fr   3 fr

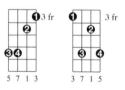

Dbmaj7#5

#5 1 3 7   1 3 #5 7
7 fr   10 fr

Dbmaj7b5

b5 7 1 3   3 7 1 b5
3 fr   3 fr

Dbmaj9

7 9 3 1   1 9 3 7
8 fr   8 fr

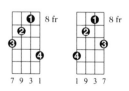

Db

Dbmaj13

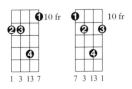

Dbm7

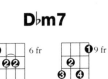

Dbm(maj7)

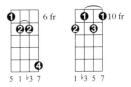

Dbm7b5

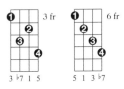

Dbm9

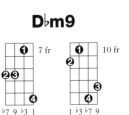

Dbm11

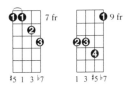

Db7

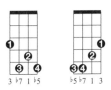

Db7sus4

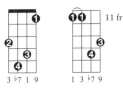

Db+7

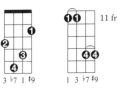

Db7b5

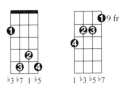

Db9

Db7#9

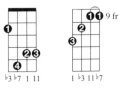

Db11

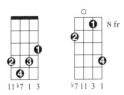

Db13

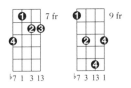

Db°7

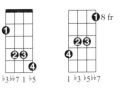

D

D

1 3 5 1   5 1 3 5

Dm

1 5 1 ♭3   5 1 ♭3 5

D+

1 3 ♯5 1   3 ♯5 1 3

D°

1 ♭5 1 ♭3   ♭5 1 ♭3 ♭5

D5
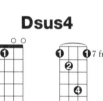

1 5 5 1   5 1 5

Dadd9
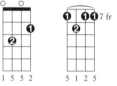

1 3 5 9   3 5 1 9

Dm(add9)
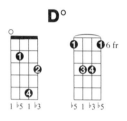

9 5 1 ♭3   1 9 ♭3 5

Dsus4

1 4 5 1   5 1 4 5

Dsus2

1 5 5 2   5 1 2 5

D6

1 5 6 3   3 6 1 5

Dm6
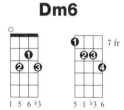

1 5 6 ♭3   5 1 ♭3 6

Dmaj7

1 5 7 3   3 7 1 5

Dmaj7♯5
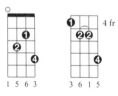

1 ♯5 7 3   ♯5 1 3 7

Dmaj7♭5
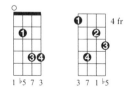

1 ♭5 7 3   3 7 1 ♭5

Dmaj9
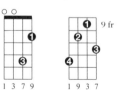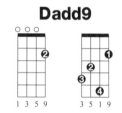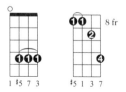

1 3 7 9   1 9 3 7

D

Dmaj13

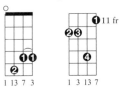

1 13 7 3   1 3 13 7

Dm7

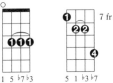

1 5 ♭7 ♭3   5 1 ♭3 ♭7

Dm(maj7)

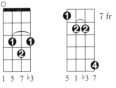

1 5 7 ♭3   5 1 ♭3 7

Dm7♭5

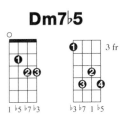

1 ♭5 ♭7 ♭3   ♭3 ♭7 1 ♭5

Dm9

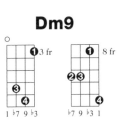

1 ♭7 9 ♭3   ♭7 9 ♭3 1

Dm11

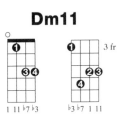

1 11 ♭7 ♭3   ♭3 ♭7 1 11

D7

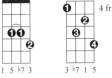

1 5 ♭7 3   3 ♭7 1 5

D7sus4

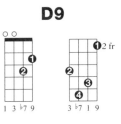

1 5 ♭7 4   4 ♭7 1 5

D+7

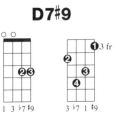

1 ♯5 ♭7 3   ♯5 1 3 ♭7

D7♭5

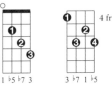

1 ♭5 ♭7 3   3 ♭7 1 ♭5

D9

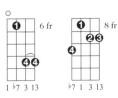

1 3 ♭7 9   3 ♭7 1 9

D7♯9

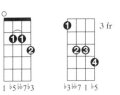

1 3 ♭7 ♯9   3 ♭7 1 ♯9

D11

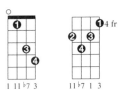

1 11 ♭7 3   11 ♭7 1 3

D13

1 ♭7 3 13   ♭7 1 3 13

D°7

1 ♭5 ♭♭7 ♭3   ♭3 ♭♭7 1 ♭5

E♭

E♭

1 3 5 1   3 5 1 3

E♭m

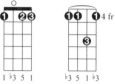

1 ♭3 5 1   ♭3 5 1 ♭3

E♭+
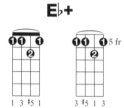

1 3 ♯5 1   3 ♯5 1 3

E♭°

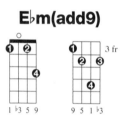

1 ♭3 ♭5 1   ♭5 1 ♭3 ♭5

E♭5
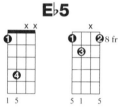

1 5   5 1 5

E♭add9
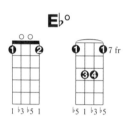

1 3 5 9   3 5 1 9

E♭m(add9)
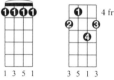

1 ♭3 5 9   9 5 1 ♭3

E♭sus4
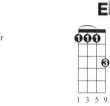

1 4 5 1   4 5 1 4

E♭sus2
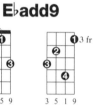

1 5 5 2   5 1 2 5

E♭6

1 3 6 1   3 6 1 5

E♭m6

1 5 6 ♭3   5 1 ♭3 6

E♭maj7
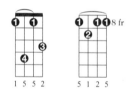

1 3 5 7   3 7 1 5

E♭maj7♯5
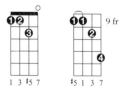

1 3 ♯5 7   ♯5 1 3 7

E♭maj7♭5

1 3 ♭5 7   3 7 1 ♭5

E♭maj9
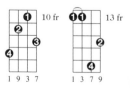

1 9 3 7   1 3 7 9

E♭

E♭maj13

1 3 13 7   7 3 13 1

E♭m7
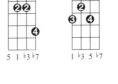

5 1 ♭3 ♭7   1 ♭3 5 ♭7

E♭m(maj7)

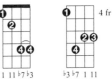

1 ♭3 5 7   5 1 ♭3 7

E♭m7♭5
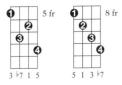

♭3 ♭5 ♭7 1   ♭5 ♭7 1 ♭3

E♭m9

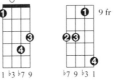

1 ♭3 ♭7 9   ♭7 9 ♭3 1

E♭m11
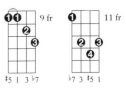

1 11 ♭7 ♭3   ♭3 ♭7 1 11

E♭7
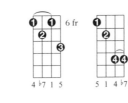

3 ♭7 1 5   5 1 3 ♭7

E♭7sus4

4 ♭7 1 5   5 1 4 ♭7

E♭+7

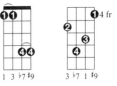

♯5 1 3 ♭7   ♭7 3 ♯5 1

E♭7♭5
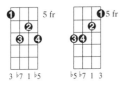

3 ♭7 1 ♭5   ♭5 ♭7 1 3

E♭9

1 3 ♭7 9   3 ♭7 1 9

E♭7♯9

1 3 ♭7 ♯9   3 ♭7 1 ♯9

E♭11
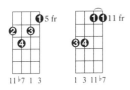

11 ♭7 1 3   1 3 11 ♭7

E♭13

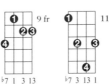

♭7 1 3 13   ♭7 3 13 1

E♭°7
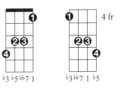

♭3 ♭5 ♭♭7 1   ♭3 ♭♭7 1 ♭5

87

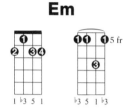

E

1 3 5 1   3 5 1 3

Em

1 ♭3 5 1   ♭3 5 1 ♭3

E+

1 3 ♯5 1   3 ♯5 1 3

E°

1 ♭3 ♭5 1   ♭5 1 ♭3 ♭5

E5

1 5 1   5 1 5

Eadd9

1 3 5 9   3 5 1 9

Em(add9)

1 ♭3 5 9   9 5 1 ♭3

Esus4

1 4 5 1   4 5 1 4

Esus2

1 2 5 1   5 1 2 5

E6

1 3 6 1   3 6 1 5

Em6

1 5 6 ♭3   5 1 ♭3 6

Emaj7

1 3 5 7   3 7 1 5

Emaj7♯5

1 3 ♯5 7   ♯5 1 3 7

Emaj7♭5

1 3 ♭5 7   3 7 1 ♭5

Emaj9

3 9 7 1   1 9 3 7

E

Emaj13
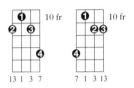

Em7

Em(maj7)
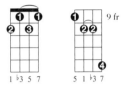

Em7♭5
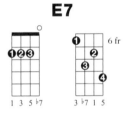

Em9
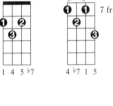

Em11
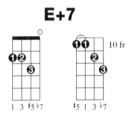

E7
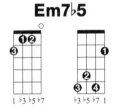

E7sus4

E+7
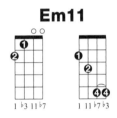

E7♭5
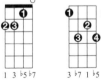

E9
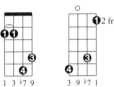

E7♯9
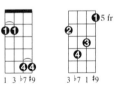

E11
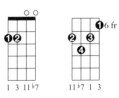

E13

E°7
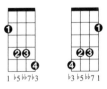

F

F

1 3 5 1   3 5 1 3

Fm

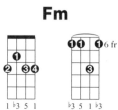

1 ♭3 5 1   ♭3 5 1 ♭3

F+

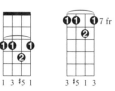

1 3 ♯5 1   3 ♯5 1 3

F°

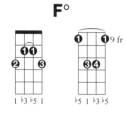

1 ♭3 ♭5 1   ♭5 1 ♭3 ♭5

F5

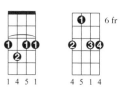

1 5 1   5 1 5

Fadd9

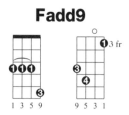

1 3 5 9   9 5 3 1

Fm(add9)

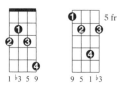

1 ♭3 5 9   9 5 1 ♭3

Fsus4

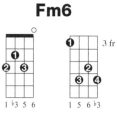

1 4 5 1   4 5 1 4

Fsus2

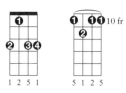

1 2 5 1   5 1 2 5

F6

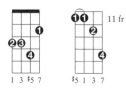

1 3 5 6   1 3 6 1

Fm6

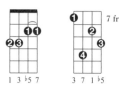

1 ♭3 5 6   1 5 6 ♭3

Fmaj7

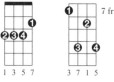

1 3 5 7   3 7 1 5

Fmaj7♯5

1 3 ♯5 7   ♯5 1 3 7

Fmaj7♭5

1 3 ♭5 7   3 7 1 ♭5

Fmaj9

7 9 3 1   1 9 3 7

F

Fmaj13

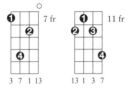

Fm7

Fm(maj7)

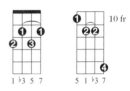

Fm7♭5

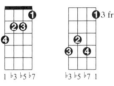

Fm9

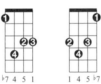

Fm11

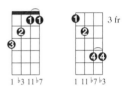

F7

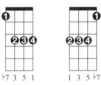

F7sus4

F+7

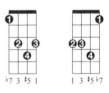

F7♭5

F9

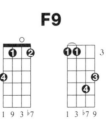

F7#9

F11

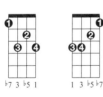

F13

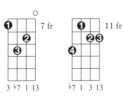

F°7

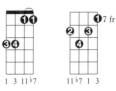

91

F#

F#
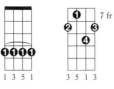

7 fr

1 3 5 1   3 5 1 3

F#m

7 fr

1 ♭3 5 1   ♭3 5 1 ♭3

F#+

1 3 #5 #5   1 3 #5 1

F#°

10 fr

1 ♭3 ♭5 1   ♭5 1 ♭3 ♭5

F#5

11 fr

1 1 5 1   5 1   5

F#add9

4 fr   4 fr

1 3 5 9   9 1 5 3

F#m(add9)
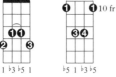

3 fr   4 fr

1 ♭3 5 9   1 5 ♭3 9

F#sus4

7 fr

1 4 5 1   4 5 1 4

F#sus2

4 fr

1 2 5 1   2 1 5 1

F#6

4 fr   8 fr

1 3 6 1   3 6 1 5

F#m6

4 fr

1 ♭3 5 6   1 5 6 ♭3

F#maj7

8 fr

1 3 5 7   3 7 1 5

F#maj7#5

8 fr

1 3 #5 7   3 7 1 #5

F#maj7♭5

8 fr

1 3 ♭5 7   3 7 1 ♭5

F#maj9

6 fr

7 9 3 1   9 1 7 3

F#maj13

13 1 3 7 | 7 1 3 13

F#m7

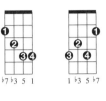

♭7 ♭3 5 1 | 1 ♭3 5 ♭7

F#m(maj7)

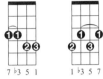

7 ♭3 5 1 | 1 ♭3 5 7

F#m7♭5

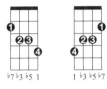

♭7 ♭3 ♭5 1 | 1 ♭3 ♭5 ♭7

F#m9

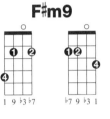

1 9 ♭3 ♭7 | ♭7 9 ♭3 1

F#m11

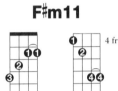

1 ♭3 11 ♭7 | 1 11 ♭7 ♭3

F#7

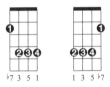

♭7 3 5 1 | 1 3 5 ♭7

F#7sus4

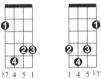

♭7 4 5 1 | 1 4 5 ♭7

F#+7

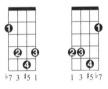

♭7 3 #5 1 | 1 3 #5 ♭7

F#7♭5

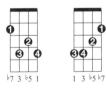

♭7 3 ♭5 1 | 1 3 ♭5 ♭7

F#9

1 3 ♭7 9 | 9 1 ♭7 3

F#7#9

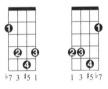

1 3 ♭7 #9 | #9 1 ♭7 3

F#11

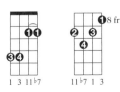

1 3 11 ♭7 | 11 ♭7 1 3

F#13

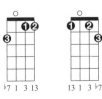

♭7 1 3 13 | 13 1 3 ♭7

F#°7

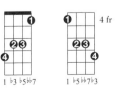

1 ♭3 ♭5 ♭7 | 1 ♭5 ♭♭7 ♭3

93

G

G

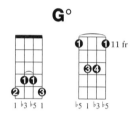

5 1 3 5   1 3 5 1

Gm

5 1 ♭3 5   1 ♭3 5 1

G+

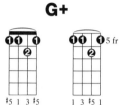

♯5 1 3 ♯5   1 3 ♯5 1

G°

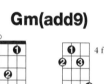

1 ♭3 ♭5 1   ♭5 1 ♭3 ♭5

G5

5 1   1 5 1

Gadd9

5 9 3 1   1 3 5 9

Gm(add9)

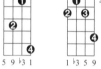

5 9 ♭3 1   1 ♭3 5 9

Gsus4

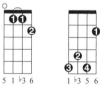

5 1 4 5   1 4 5 1

Gsus2

5 1 2 5   1 2 5 1

G6

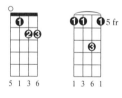

5 1 3 6   1 3 6 1

Gm6

5 1 ♭3 6   1 ♭3 5 6

Gmaj7

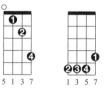

5 1 3 7   1 3 5 7

Gmaj7♯5

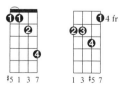

♯5 1 3 7   1 3 ♯5 7

Gmaj7♭5

1 3 ♭5 7   3 7 1 ♭5

Gmaj9

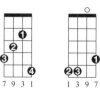

7 9 3 1   1 3 9 7

G

Gmaj13
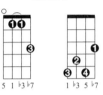

Gm7

Gm(maj7)
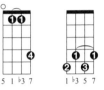

Gm7♭5
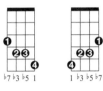

Gm9
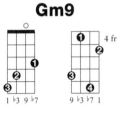

Gm11
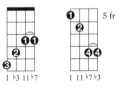

G7

G7sus4
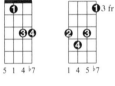

G+7
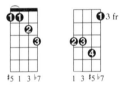

G7♭5
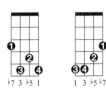

G9
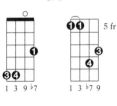

G7#9
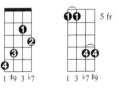

G11
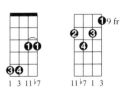

G13

G°7
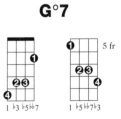

A♭

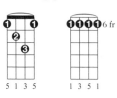

5 1 3 5   1 3 5 1

A♭m

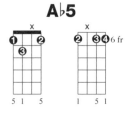

5 1 ♭3 5   1 ♭3 5 1

A♭+

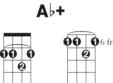

♯5 1 3 ♯5   1 3 ♯5 1

A♭°

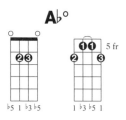

♭5 1 ♭3 ♭5   1 ♭3 ♭5 1

A♭5

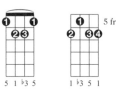

5 1 5   1 5 1

A♭add9

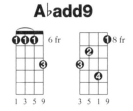

1 3 5 9   3 5 1 9

A♭m(add9)

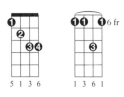

1 ♭3 5 9   ♭3 5 1 9

A♭sus4

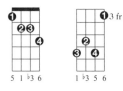

5 1 4 5   1 4 5 1

A♭sus2

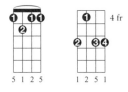

5 1 2 5   1 2 5 1

A♭6

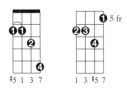

5 1 3 6   1 3 6 1

A♭m6

5 1 ♭3 6   1 ♭3 5 6

A♭maj7

1 3 5 7   3 7 1 5

A♭maj7♯5

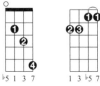

♯5 1 3 7   1 3 ♯5 7

A♭maj7♭5

♭5 1 3 7   1 3 ♭5 7

A♭maj9

7 9 3 1   1 3 7 9

A♭

A♭maj13
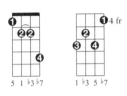

A♭m7
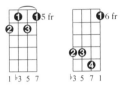

A♭m(maj7)
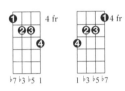

A♭m7♭5
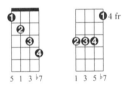

A♭m9
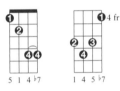

A♭m11
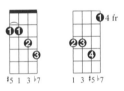

A♭7
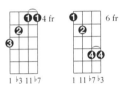

A♭7sus4

A♭+7
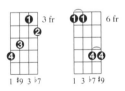

A♭7♭5

A♭9

A♭7#9

A♭11
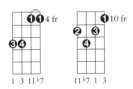

A♭13

A♭°7
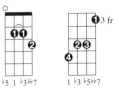

97

Open D

A

A
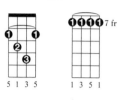

Am
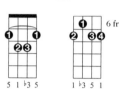

A+
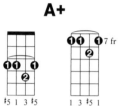

A°
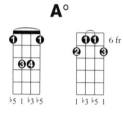

A5
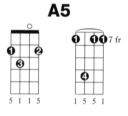

Aadd9
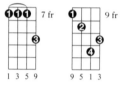

Am(add9)
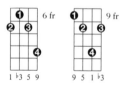

Asus4
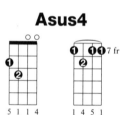

Asus2
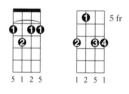

A6
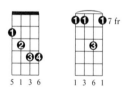

Am6
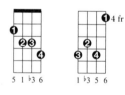

Amaj7
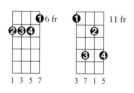

Amaj7♯5
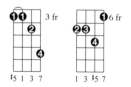

Amaj7♭5
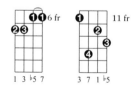

Amaj9
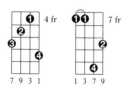

98

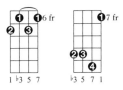

A

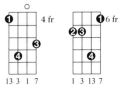 Amaj13

Am7

Am(maj7)

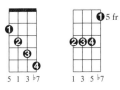 Am7♭5

 Am9

 Am11

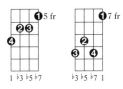 A7

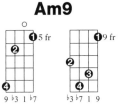 A7sus4

 A+7

A7♭5

A9

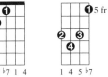 A7#9

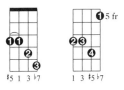 A11

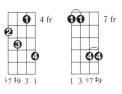 A13

A°7

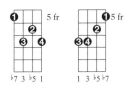

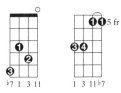   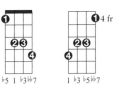

B♭

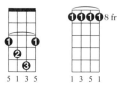

B♭m

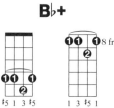

B♭+

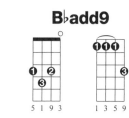

B♭°

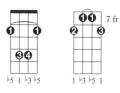

B♭5

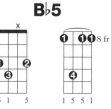

B♭add9

B♭m(add9)

B♭sus4

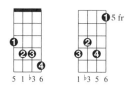

B♭sus2

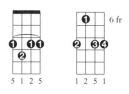

B♭6

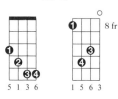

B♭m6

B♭maj7

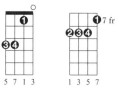

B♭maj7♯5

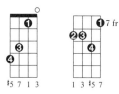

B♭maj7♭5

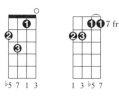

B♭maj9

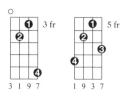

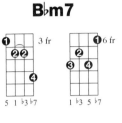

B♭maj13

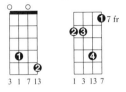

3 1 7 13   1 3 13 7

B♭m7

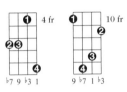

5 1 ♭3 ♭7   1 ♭3 5 ♭7

B♭m(maj7)

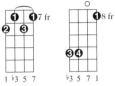

1 ♭3 5 7   ♭3 5 7 1

B♭m7♭5

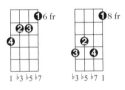

1 ♭3 ♭5 ♭7   ♭3 ♭5 ♭7 1

B♭m9

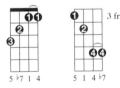

♭7 9 ♭3 1   9 ♭7 1 ♭3

B♭m11

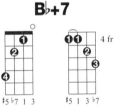

1 ♭3 11 ♭7   ♭3 ♭7 1 11

B♭7

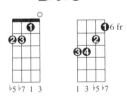

5 ♭7 1 3   5 1 3 ♭7

B♭7sus4

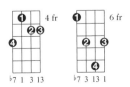

5 ♭7 1 4   5 1 4 ♭7

B♭+7

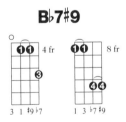

♯5 ♭7 1 3   ♯5 1 3 ♭7

B♭7♭5

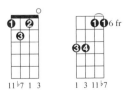

♭5 ♭7 1 3   1 3 ♭5 ♭7

B♭9

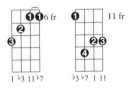

♭7 1 9 3   1 3 ♭7 9

B♭7♯9

3 1 ♯9 ♭7   1 3 ♭7 ♯9

B♭11

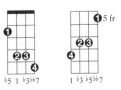

11 ♭7 1 3   1 3 11 ♭7

B♭13

♭7 1 3 13   ♭7 3 13 1

B♭°7

♭5 1 ♭3 ♭♭7   1 ♭3 ♭5 ♭♭7

B

3 5 1 3   5 1 3 5

Bm

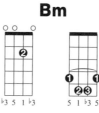

♭3 5 1 ♭3   5 1 ♭3 5

B+

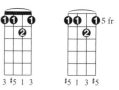

3 ♯5 1 3   ♯5 1 3 ♯5

B°

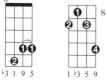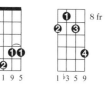

♭5 1 ♭3 ♭5   1 ♭3 ♭5 1

B5

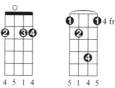

5 5 1 5   1   5 1

Badd9

1 3 5 9   9 5 1 3

Bm(add9)

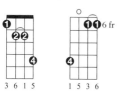

♭3 1 9 5   1 ♭3 5 9

Bsus4

4 5 1 4   5 1 4 5

Bsus2

5 1 2 5   1 2 5 1

B6

3 6 1 5   1 5 3 6

Bm6

♭3 6 1 5   5 1 ♭3 6

Bmaj7

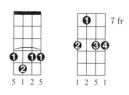

5 7 1 3   1 3 5 7

Bmaj7♯5

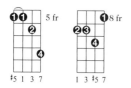

♯5 1 3 7   1 3 ♯5 7

Bmaj7♭5

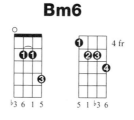

♭5 7 1 3   1 3 ♭5 7

Bmaj9

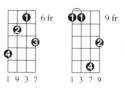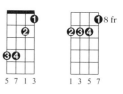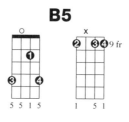

1 9 3 7   1 3 7 9

B

Bmaj13
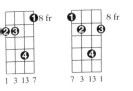

1 3 13 7   7 3 13 1

Bm7

⌀ 7 fr

♭3 ♭7 1 5   1 ♭3 5 ♭7

Bm(maj7)
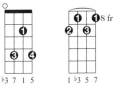

♭3 7 1 5   1 ♭3 5 7

Bm7♭5
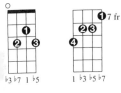

♭3 ♭7 1 ♭5   1 ♭3 5 ♭7

Bm9
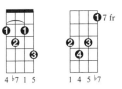

♭3 1 9 ♭7   ♭7 9 ♭3 1

Bm11

♭3 ♭7 1 11   1 ♭3 11 ♭7

B7

3 ♭7 1 5   1 3 5 ♭7

B7sus4
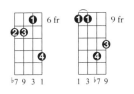

4 ♭7 1 5   1 4 5 ♭7

B+7

♯5 1 3 ♭7   1 3 ♯5 ♭7

B7♭5
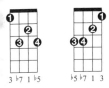

3 ♭7 1 ♭5   ♭5 ♭7 1 3

B9

♭7 9 3 1   1 3 ♭7 9

B7♯9
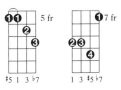

3 ♭7 1 ♯9   1 3 ♭7 ♯9

B11
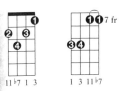

11 ♭7 1 3   1 3 11 ♭7

B13
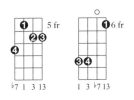

♭7 1 3 13   1 3 ♭7 13

B°7
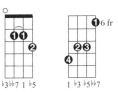

♭3 ♭♭7 1 ♭5   1 ♭3 ♭5 ♭♭7

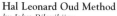